THE
PASSIONATE
INTELLECT

Christian Faith and the
Discipleship of the Mind

ALISTER MCGRATH

IVP Books

An imprint of InterVarsity Press
Downers Grove, Illinois

InterVarsity Press
P.O. Box 1400, Downers Grove, IL 60515-1426
World Wide Web: www.ivpress.com
E-mail: email@ivpress.com

Published in the United States of America by InterVarsity Press, Downers Grove, Illinois, with permission from SPCK Publishing, London, England.

InterVarsity Press® is the book-publishing division of InterVarsity Christian Fellowship/USA®, a movement of students and faculty active on campus at hundreds of universities, colleges and schools of nursing in the United States of America, and a member movement of the International Fellowship of Evangelical Students. For information about local and regional activities, write Public Relations Dept., InterVarsity Christian Fellowship/USA, 6400 Schroeder Rd., P.O. Box 7895, Madison, WI 53707-7895, or visit the IVCF website at <www.intervarsity.org>.

All Scripture quotations, unless otherwise indicated, are taken from the Holy Bible, New International Version®. NIV®. Copyright ©1973, 1978, 1984 by International Bible Society. Used by permission of Zondervan Publishing House. All rights reserved.

Design: Cindy Kiple
Images: Qweek/iStockphoto

ISBN 978-0-8308-3843-1 (hardcover)
ISBN 978-0-8308-3675-8 (paperback)

Printed in the United States of America ∞

Library of Congress Cataloging-in-Publication Data

McGrath, Alister E., 1953-
  The passionate intellect: Christian faith and the discipleship of the mind / Alister McGrath.
      p. cm.
  Includes bibliographical references and index.
  ISBN 978-0-8308-3843-1 (cloth: alk. paper)
  1. Theology. I. Title.
  BT75.3.M337 2010
  230—dc22

                                                              2010014321

P	18	17	16	15	14	13	12	11	10	9	8	7	6	5	4	3	2	1
Y	29	28	27	26	25	24	23	22	21	20	19	18	17	16	15	14

CONTENTS

INTRODUCTION

Christian theology is one of the most intellectually stimulating and exciting subjects it is possible to study, rich in resources for the life of faith and the ministry of the church. It has the capacity to excite, inspire and illuminate the human intellect, giving it a new passion and focus.[1] Affirming and celebrating the intellectual resilience and vigor of faith is not about downplaying, still less denying, its many other aspects—such as the nurturing of a relationship with God, sustained by prayer, reflection and adoration. This book may be seen both as an intellectual defense of the place of theology in the Christian life, and as a plea for the Christian church to take the life of the mind seriously, especially in the light of contemporary public debates.

This book is about "mere theology," a phrase I have shamelessly borrowed and adapted from C. S. Lewis's famous notion of "mere Christianity."[2] By "mere theology," I mean the basic themes that have characterized the Christian vision of reality down the ages. This book does not defend or advocate any particular school or style of theology, but rather sets out to explore how the great tradition of Christian theological reflection enriches our faith and deepens our engagement with the concerns and debates of the world around us. While Lewis is a well-known representative of this approach, it extends far beyond (and behind) him. All too often, theology merely generates controversy and factionalism within the church. My concern here is to focus on the positive role of theology in shaping, nourishing and safeguarding the Christian vision of reality, and applying it to the challenges and opportunities that Christians face today.

It may be helpful if I set this book in context. The last couple of years have been very significant in my life, both in terms of events and scholarship. After exactly twenty-five years' service to the Faculty of Theology at Oxford University, I took up the newly established Chair of Theology, Ministry and Education at King's College, London, in September 2008. King's College was founded by King George IV and the Duke of Wellington in 1829 to encourage a creative interaction between the academy, church and society, and has a long tradition of fostering theological engagement and reflection. Although I am an academic theologian, I have always believed that theology is at its best when it generates reflective practices in the life and service of the church. The new London chair was set up to encourage a direct engagement between theology and the life of the church, and I count myself deeply privileged to be its first occupant.

Earlier in 2008 I gave the Riddell Memorial Lectures at the University of Newcastle-upon-Tyne, exploring how the new way of seeing things made possible by the Christian faith leads to a revitalization of our engagement with nature. These lectures in effect represented a manifesto for a new style of natural theology, firmly grounded in the Christian tradition.[3]

In the 2009 Gifford Lectures at the ancient University of Aberdeen, I followed through this new approach, focusing on the theological and apologetic significance of phenomena of "fine-tuning" in nature.[4] Finally, I delivered the 2009-2010 Hulsean Lectures at the University of Cambridge, taking as my theme the implications of Darwinism for a Christian natural theology.[5] Some of the themes of these lectures are echoed in this volume.

Yet the book as a whole reflects a wider cultural background. In 2006 the movement now widely, if inaccurately, known as the new atheism exploded on the cultural scene. Richard Dawkins's *God Delusion* (2006), Daniel Dennett's *Breaking the Spell* (2006) and Christopher Hitchens's *God Is Not Great* (2007) created a media fascination with religion and its discontents. Public interest in the God question soared. I found myself regularly being called upon to speak and write on these themes[6] and debate leading atheists in public: Richard Dawkins in Oxford, Daniel Dennett in London and Christopher Hitchens in Washington. Although I much prefer seminar rooms to debating chambers, there was no doubt that the issues being contested were a matter of general, not just academic, interest. To my surprise, I found that I had become a public intellectual.

Debate often centered on the rationality of faith and the coherence of the Christian vision of reality. For the new atheists Christianity represents an antiquated way of explaining things that can be pensioned off in the modern scientific age. In one of the wonderfully unsubstantiated assertions that make up so much of his case against religion, Christopher Hitchens tells us that since the invention of the telescope and microscope religion "no longer offers an explanation of anything important."[7] It's a nice sound bite which, when placed alongside many other equally unsubstantiated sound bites, almost manages to create the semblance of an evidence-based argument. But is it anything more than that?

In his brilliantly argued critique of the new atheism, Terry Eagleton ridicules those who treat religion as a purely explanatory matter. "Christianity was never meant to be an explanation of anything in the first place. It's rather like saying that thanks to the electric toaster we can forget about Chekhov." Believing that religion is a "botched attempt to explain the world" is on the same intellectual level as "seeing ballet as a botched attempt to run for a bus."[8]

Eagleton is surely right here. There is far more to Christianity than an attempt to make sense of things. The New Testament is primarily concerned with the transformation of human existence through the life, death and resurrection of Jesus of Nazareth. The gospel is thus not so much about explanation as about salvation—the transformation of the human situation. Yet while the emphasis of the Christian proclamation may not be on explaining the world, it nevertheless also offers a distinctive way of looking at things which, at least in principle, enables us to see things in different ways and thus leads us to act in ways consistent with this. Christianity involves believing that certain things are true, that they may be relied upon and that they illuminate our perceptions, decisions and actions. These themes are essential to "mere theology," and they feature prominently in this manifesto for the reasonableness of faith.

The public debate about the rationality of faith continued in 2009, a year which marked the two hundredth anniversary of the birth of Charles Darwin (1809-1882), the great English naturalist and founder of modern evolutionary thought, as well as the 150th anniversary of the publication of his ground-breaking *The Origin of Species*. The cultural importance of Darwin was such that these celebrations quite eclipsed other anniversaries marked during that year, including the five-hundredth anniversary of the birth of John Calvin (1509-1564).[9] Darwin's anniversary was seized upon by many in the new atheism as a means of advocating a secularist agenda by associating it (in this case rather implausibly) with this scientific hero. As one of the relatively few theologians who knew a lot about both Darwin and evolutionary theory, I found myself once more thrust into public debate about the religious, moral and cultural implications of Darwin's ideas.

This book reflects these broader cultural concerns, which are likely to remain important for some time to come. In addition to exploring the integrity and vitality of Christian theology, the volume emphasises its capacity for robust intellectual and cultural engagement. There is a growing consensus that the sudden development of the new atheism took the churches by surprise during this period. They were, it seems, intellectually unprepared for this major new challenge. There are now welcome signs that the new atheism is fading in its appeal and profile, not least on account of some robust and penetrating analysis by leading authorities of its unreliable critiques of religion on the one hand,[10] and its deficient proposed secular alternatives on the other. Yet the best preparation for the next crisis of confidence, whatever form it may take, is to encourage the emergence of an informed and confident life of the mind within the churches—something that this work is intended to stimulate.

The Passionate Intellect consists of eleven chapters, based on previously unpublished lectures and addresses, given in various North American and European locations over a two-year period from late 2007 to late 2009. (See the notes section at the end of the book for further details.) The volume is arranged thematically. Its first six chapters deal with the purpose, place and relevance of Christian theology. Their common theme is the intellectual capaciousness of the Christian faith and its ability to bring about a new and deeply satisfying vision of reality. Christianity is celebrated as something that both makes sense in itself and has the capacity to make sense of many other aspects of reality as well. I often cite C. S. Lewis's famous words in public debates when making this point: "I believe in Christianity as I believe that the Sun has risen—not only because I see it, but because by it, I see everything else."[11] As a "discipleship of the mind," Christian theology leads to a deeper appreciation of the capacity of the gospel to engage with the complexities of the natural world on the one hand and human experience on the other. At the same time, we must realize that theology has its limits, which must be identified and respected.

The opening two chapters offer a general introduction to the study of theology, which I hope will be particularly useful for those looking for some guidance on how to begin their reflections. Theology is presented here as a positive, critical and constructive discipline concerned to inform and sustain the Christian vision of reality—something that is essential to Christian ministry and preaching. These chapters are designed to help those who are new to the study of theology to orientate themselves and get a sense of their bearings as they navigate the field.

In chapter three I explore George Herbert's poem "The Elixir," which was first published in 1633 and remains one of the finest theological accounts of the transformation of vision, evaluation and action that ensues from the Christian faith. The poem illustrates a leading theme of "mere theology"—its positive role in transforming the way we see things, leading to an enriched perception of reality and a deeper sense of our own possibilities and responsibilities within the world.

Next we look at a complex and unsettling topic, often neglected. What happens when there is a tension between theory and experience? The fourth chapter considers the quite different approaches to theological ambiguity found in Martin Luther and C. S. Lewis, noting their significance for the life of faith.

The fifth chapter considers what difference the Christian faith makes to the way we see the natural world and behave toward it. How does it stand up in comparison with its atheist and pagan alternatives? Chapter six deals with the link between theology and apologetics. In what way can theology enable the church to affirm the credibility and attractiveness of faith in contemporary culture? To engage in dialogue and debate in the public square? This traditional question has become more important in the light of recent atheist writings, making it all the more essential to ensure that the church builds and sustains its witness upon firm and reliable theological foundations.

Having laid the ground for a theologically informed engagement with culture, the remainder of the book explores how inhabiting the Christian "interpretive community" provides a platform for cultural engagement.[12] The Christian gospel mandates a vibrant engagement with our culture, not an isolationist withdrawal from it. Christians are called to be salt and light to the world (Matthew 5:13-16). A theologically informed discipleship of the mind sustains, nourishes and protects the Christian vision of reality, thus enabling the church to retain its saltiness and capacity to illuminate. Yet this is the precondition for cultural engagement, not a substitute for it. Theology energizes and enables the church to witness in the public square, helping it to frame its compelling intellectual, moral and spiritual vision of reality.

This section opens with a chapter considering the Christian engagement with the natural sciences, often inaccurately presented as being locked in mortal conflict with the Christian faith. Exploring the relation of Christian belief and the natural sciences has long impressed me as significant. My own journey of faith involved extended reflections on these questions, which remain important for many today. Here I offer what I believe to be theologically and scientifically informed responses to some contemporary concerns and questions, which are often of particular significance to Christian students of the natural sciences.

Chapters eight and nine explore some of the religious implications of Darwinism. The Darwin anniversary year (2009) led to intense media interest in the relation of Darwin and faith, often linked with the repeated and highly questionable assertion that Darwin's ideas discredited Christianity. In rebutting such suggestions chapter eight looks specifically at the place of faith—both scientific and religious—in Darwin's reflections on natural selection. Chapter nine sets out the relation of creation and evolution in the thought of Augustine of Hippo (354-430), offering some timely reflections for contemporary debates.

Darwin, of course, has been adopted as a mascot by many within the new atheism. The final two chapters of the book deal with the origins, pedigree and intellectual integrity of this movement. Chapter ten considers whether the visceral antagonism of the new atheism toward religion can be taken seriously, and offers some reflections on how a more civilized discussion of the issues might take place. This chapter explores the "rhetoric of dismissal" of religion, which is characteristic of writers such as Christopher Hitchens. I contrast it with the very different findings of mainline scholarship on a variety of issues, such as the origins of totalitarianism, the motivations of suicide bombers and the problem of fanatical violence. In particular, I criticize the notion of the "Brights," introduced in 2003, as a less than subtle affirmation of the alleged intellectual superiority of atheists over religious believers.

Finally, chapter eleven looks carefully and critically at one of the most important yet understudied aspects of the new atheism: the observation that far from being something "new," it is actually deeply rooted in the assumptions of the eighteenth-century Enlightenment. Its aggressiveness and dogmatism may indeed be new; its leading ideas are recycled from the past. Appreciating this connection casts light on some of the leading features of this form of atheism, especially its extraordinary hostility toward postmodernism. Can a movement so deeply embedded in the assumptions of a past age meet the challenges of our postmodern era? And what can the churches learn from this?

I hope that this short work will further stimulate the development of the discipleship of the mind within the churches and enrich our vision of the Christian faith. Every chapter in this work had its origins as a public lecture, a seminar paper or a presentation to a small group of people, often students. Each has been completely rewritten to take account of the questions raised by their audiences. I am deeply grateful to those audiences for their interactions. Recrafting and redrafting is not something authors enjoy; nevertheless, it is essential if we are to connect with where people really are, rather than where we hope they might be. I also acknowledge with pleasure the editorial skills of Alison Barr and Lauren Chiosso, which proved so helpful in bringing this work to completion.

PART ONE

THE PURPOSE, PLACE AND RELEVANCE OF CHRISTIAN THEOLOGY

MERE THEOLOGY

The Landscape of Faith 1

FAITH IS FUNDAMENTALLY a relational matter; it is about trusting God.[1] Yet part of the inner dynamic of the life of faith is a desire to understand more about who and what we trust. Anselm of Canterbury (c. 1033-1109) famously remarked that theology is basically "faith seeking understanding." The great Christian theologian Augustine of Hippo (354-430) was also clear that there is a genuine intellectual excitement to wrestling with God. Theology is a passion of the mind, a longing to understand more about God's nature and ways, and the transformative impact that this has on life. Our faith can be deepened and our personal lives enriched through theological reflection. So how do we set about developing this passion of the mind?

We cannot explore the relevance of theology, however, without first noting how bad a reputation it has developed within the churches in the last few decades. For some Christian leaders theology is irrelevant to real life. It is about retreating into ivory towers when there are more pressing things to worry about. Yet rightly understood, theology is about enabling informed Christian action. It makes us *want* to do things, and do them in a Christian way. It helps us make judgments about how best to act; it encourages us to engage with the real world.

Other Christian leaders express anxiety concerning the tendency of theology to create division and conflict within the church. J. I. Packer, one of evangelicalism's most influential and wise voices, has written of the problem of "entrenched intellectualists"—"rigid, argumentative, critical Christians, champions of God's truth for whom orthodoxy is all." I think we all know people who seem to have an obsession with what Packer calls "winning the battle for mental correctness" and little interest in any other aspect of the Christian faith. They may love God, but they seem to have problems loving other people—especially when they disagree with them. It's not always easy to discern how this fixation on theological correctness links up with the Gospel accounts of the ministry of Jesus of Nazareth. Surely the better way is to pursue a generous orthodoxy, seeing disagreements in the context of the greater agreements which bind us together?

The heartbeat of the Christian faith lies in the sheer intellectual delight and excitement caused by the person of Jesus of Nazareth. Here is someone who the church finds to be intellectually luminous, spiritually persuasive and infinitely satisfying, both communally and individually. While Christians express this delight and wonder in their creeds, they do so more especially in their worship and adoration. Centuries ago, Augustine of Hippo reflected on the way in which communities were unified by the objects of their love. The surest way of enhancing the identity, coherence and cohesion of a community is to help it see what it loves more clearly, and thence to love it more dearly.

That is why worship is so important for Christian identity. It focuses our attention on what really matters, and proclaims that the Christian faith has the power to capture the imagination—not merely to persuade the mind—by throwing open the depths of the human soul to the realities of the gospel. It sustains a great passion for Jesus Christ, which nourishes the theological task even as it calls into question its capacity to live up to the brilliance of its ultimate object.

Yet while the appeal of the Christian vision of Jesus of Nazareth to the baptized imagination and emotions must never be neglected or understated, we need to appreciate that there remains an intellectual core to the Christian faith. We cannot love God without wanting to understand more about him. We are called upon to love God with our minds, as well as our hearts and souls (Matthew 22:37). We cannot allow Christ to reign in our hearts if he does not also guide our thinking. The discipleship of the mind is just as important as any other part of the process by which we grow in our faith and commitment.

The defense of the intellectual credibility of Christianity has become increasingly important in recent years, not least on account of the rise of the new atheism. We must see ourselves as standard-bearers for the spiritual, ethical, imaginative and intellectual vitality of the Christian faith, working out why we believe that certain things are true and what difference they make to the way we live our lives and engage with the world around us. Above all, we must expand our vision of the Christian gospel. For some, realizing how much more there is to know about our faith can seem intimidating. But it can also be exciting to anticipate the discoveries that lie ahead, as the rich landscape of the Christian faith unfolds before our eyes.

Let us explore this image of the "landscape of faith" a little further. Imagine that you are standing on a mountain ridge. Below you, spread out like a tapestry, is a beautiful landscape, stretching into the far distance. Woods, streams, fields, villages are all lit by the gentle radiance of a late afternoon sun. It's the sort of thing that made Romantics like William Wordsworth want to rush off and write poetry. So how would you describe such a stunning vista to a friend back home?

It's actually quite hard to do this, except in the most superficial way, because words are just not good enough to express our experience of reality. You could tell your friend that you saw a wood—but that little word *wood* is never going to convey your vibrant memory of a green mass of trees, their dappled leaves shimmering in the sunlight and your emotional reaction to such beauty.

You could draw a map of the landscape, which helps you see how its elements related to each other—woods, mountains, streams and villages. But it was not a map that moved you to wonder and delight, but the landscape itself—the beautiful view, the cool wind, the fragrance of flowers and resin, the distant tinkling of cowbells as the herds wander around, seeking the best pastures.

It may be helpful to think of theology as a map and the gospel as a landscape. This helps us grasp that theology tries to describe in words what we encounter through faith. When we understand theology properly, it helps us articulate, deepen and communicate the Christian vision of God in all its fullness and wonder. On the other hand, when theology becomes preoccupied with the relation of ideas, it loses sight of the vision of God, which gives vitality to the life of faith. The worshiping community is the crucible in which much of the best theology is forged, even though it may be refined by academic reflection.

We will remain with the image of the landscape for a moment longer, as there is another point we need to consider. As we try to take in our vast, rich and beautiful panorama, most of us will find ourselves concentrating on one part of the view that we especially like or are particularly struck by, filtering out the rest. This "selective attention" or "cognitive bias" is helpful in some ways. It allows us to focus on what we think really matters. Yet all too often it means that we miss out on other things. We fail to see other features of the landscape or appreciate their importance.

Now imagine that you are joined by a group of friends, all looking at the same panorama. In one sense all of you will see the same view. Yet the observational dynamic is quite different. As you start talking to each other, it soon becomes clear that others have noticed things that you missed—a fork in a stream, a small lake or some cattle finding shade from the hot afternoon sun under a tree. A corporate view of the landscape emerges, which is far more comprehensive and reliable than any individual account of it. Not only will a group see *more* than any single individual; a group may also correct an individual's account of the landscape of faith. What one person thought was a stream running through a wood might actually turn out to be a trail.

The significance of this point is that we need theology to give a comprehensive, critical account of faith, rather than being limited to one individual's often very subjective perception of things. A number of theologians—such as Cyril of Jerusalem (313-386) and Vladimir Lossky (1903-1958)—have emphasised the "catholicity" of Christian theology. Their point is that the theologian is not a lone maverick but someone who works collaboratively within the body of Christ to build up a fully orbed understanding of the gospel.

We can take this a stage further. Theology values the perspectives and insights of those who have mapped and traveled the road of faith in the past, and have now arrived at their journey's end. Augustine of Hippo, Thomas Aquinas (c. 1225-1274), Martin Luther (1493-1546) and Karl Barth (1886-1968) are all dead. But they are widely recognized in theological reflection and debate today as authoritative, living voices, who have the capacity to enrich, stimulate and challenge us as we think through issues for ourselves. One of the senses of the theological term *tradition* is learning to respect those who have reflected on the great questions of theology before us. What many call "the great tradition" is both a resource and challenge to us: it puts at our disposal theological treasures that we may value and make use of today, but it also questions whether our theological generation understands and communicates the gospel as well as our forebears.

This naturally leads us to reflect on the sources of theology. Christians have quite distinct ideas about who God is and what God is like. But where do they get these ideas from? It is generally accepted that there are three major sources for theology: the Bible, reason and tradition. Each merits further discussion.

THE BIBLE

There is widespread agreement within Christianity that the Bible has a place of special importance in theological debate and personal devotion. All the major Protestant confessions of faith stress the centrality of the Bible. More recently, the Second Vatican Council (1962-1965) reaffirmed its importance for

Catholic theology and preaching. The authority of the Bible is linked with the idea of "inspiration"—in other words, that in some way, the words of the Bible convey the words of God, which all Christians regard as being of immense importance to matters of faith. Christian theology can be seen both as the *process* of reflecting on the Bible and weaving together its ideas and themes, and as the *result* of this process of reflection on certain ideas.

We must ensure that we weave *all* the Bible's themes into our thinking, not merely those we find easy to understand or we happen to like—even if this sometimes leads us to conclusions that seem deeply counterintuitive.

We can see this process of weaving a rich theological tapestry from biblical threads in the Christian understanding of Jesus of Nazareth. All the evidence we possess suggests that those who witnessed Jesus in action initially tried to interpret him in terms of existing models and categories—for example, as a healer or prophet. It was entirely natural to do so. After all, the Old Testament contained many references to God's ways of acting in the world. Why not regard Jesus as a new Elijah, a prophet who was able to heal the sick and declare God's will? But though Jesus is clearly presented in the New Testament as a human being who wept, became hungry and thirsty, and suffered and died, there was obviously more to him than this. He is referred to as *Savior*, a term laden with theological significance. Israel was absolutely clear that only God could save. To address Jesus in this way suggests he did something that only the Lord God of Israel could do. After a long process of exploring all the options, the Christian church concluded that the identity and significance of Jesus Christ could only be safeguarded and properly understood by insisting that he was truly

God and truly human. There was simply no other way of doing justice to the biblical witness to Jesus Christ.

A further example of this process of weaving is to be found in the doctrine of the Trinity. The best way of understanding this doctrine is to see it as the outcome of a process of sustained and critical reflection by Christians on the pattern of divine activity revealed in Scripture and continued in Christian experience. This is not to say that Scripture contains a doctrine of the Trinity; rather, Scripture bears witness to a God who demands to be understood in a trinitarian manner. An implicit trinitarian logic can be discerned within the New Testament, especially in its statements concerning the works of God.

The Christian Bible witnesses to the nature and actions of one God, who Christians refer to as the "God and Father of our Lord Jesus Christ." But Christianity's vision of God is rich and complex and extremely difficult to put into words. Down the ages, Christian theologians have realized that they have two basic options. They could set out a very simple concept of God, which is easily grasped but fails to do justice to the profound and multifaceted witness to God found initially in the Bible, and subsequently in Christian worship and experience. Or they could do their best to remain faithful to this witness to God—even though the end result turned out to be difficult to understand. Orthodox Christian theology has more or less always adopted the second of these two courses.

REASON

These musings on the doctrine of the Trinity also help us to begin to explore the place of reason in theology. At least on the face of it, the doctrine of the Trinity seems not to make much sense. One of my more vivid childhood memories is going to a church service in the countryside in Northern Ireland, back in the late 1950s. For reasons that I cannot entirely recall, we said the Athanasian Creed, using the traditional language of the Book of Common Prayer (1662). As we recited its rather ponderous statements, we came to affirming our belief in "the Father incomprehensible, the Son incomprehensible, and the Holy Ghost incomprehensible." I can still recall the loud voice of a slightly deaf local farmer, standing by my side, booming out "The whole damn thing's incomprehensible." The congregation, having paused for breath at that particular point, had no difficulty in hearing this piece of theological wisdom with disconcerting clarity.

Traditionally, Christian theology has seen reason as operating in a subservient role to revelation. Thomas Aquinas argued that supernatural truths needed to be revealed to us. Human reason, on its own, could not hope to gain access to divine mysteries. It could, however, reflect on them, once they had been revealed. The doctrine of the Trinity knits together into a coherent whole the Christian doctrines of creation, redemption and sanctification. By doing so, it sets before us a vision of a God who created the world and whose glory can be seen reflected in the wonders of the natural order; a God who redeemed the world, whose love can be seen in the tender face of Christ; and a God who is present now in the lives of believers. In this sense the doctrine can be said to preserve the mystery of God by ensuring that the Christian understanding of God is not impoverished through reductionism or rationalism.

REASON AND MYSTERY

Yet however important and helpful reason may be in theology, we have to acknowledge its limits in making sense of things. If we can't make sense of something, it may simply be wrong. But it might also be so profound and complex that we simply cannot comprehend it. Patristic writers regularly compared understanding God with looking directly into the sun. In much the same way as the human eye cannot cope with the brilliance of the sun, so the human mind cannot cope with the glory of God.

A conversation between the Roman emperor Hadrian and the Jewish rabbi Joshua ben Hananiah (d. 131) makes this point well. Hadrian, dismissive of Jewish theology, demanded to be shown Joshua's God. The rabbi replied that this was impossible, an answer which failed to satisfy the emperor Hadrian. Joshua therefore took the emperor outside, and asked him to stare at the midday Palestinian summer sun. "That is impossible!" replied the emperor. "If you cannot look at the sun," replied the rabbi, "how much less can you behold the glory of God, who created it?"

The idea of *mystery* is helpful here. Unfortunately, it is a word that is easily misunderstood. The language of theology sometimes seems to have little connection with the words we use in everyday life. Our definition of *hope*, for example, might be "something I would very much like to be true." The deeper theological meaning of the word as "a sure and confident expectation" is lost. We find the same problem with a word that occurs in Paul's exultant declaration that "the mystery that has been hidden throughout the ages and generations but has now been revealed to his saints" (Colossians 1:26 NRSV). What do we mean by *mystery?*

When I first began to study theology, the meaning of the word seemed obvious. I was an avid fan of detective fiction back in those days, and I regularly pored over the secondhand book stalls in Oxford's covered market, searching for Earl

Stanley Gardner novels to add to my collection. Colin Dexter's "Inspector Morse" series began to appear around this time, adding considerably to my delight, not least because it was actually set in Oxford. My theological understanding of mystery was based largely on reading crime fiction. A mystery was a puzzling series of events that could be explained by some sharp detective work.

Eventually, I realized that my understanding of mystery was inadequate and did not really correspond to what the New Testament meant by the term. As I began to wrestle with writers such as Gregory of Nyssa (335-394), it became clear to me that there was another way of understanding the idea, which made a lot more sense. Both the New Testament and Christian spiritual writers use the term *mystery* to refer to the hidden depths of the Christian faith that stretch beyond the reach of reason. To speak of God as a mystery is not to lapse into some kind of obscurantism or woolly and muddled way of thinking. It is simply to admit the limits placed on our human reason and the hold it can obtain on the living God. We are predisposed to reduce God to what we can cope with, to bring God down to our own level, to dilute God, to scale God down. Yet we ought to allow God to open our minds and enlarge our apprehension of the divine reality and glory.

We have a natural and entirely healthy instinct to resist anything that seems irrational. Yet there are some aspects of the world that human reason finds very difficult to comprehend. In his *Varieties of Religious Experience* (1902), the famous psychologist William James (1842-1910) notes that religious experience "defies expression" and cannot be described adequately in words. "Its quality must be directly experienced; it cannot be imparted or transferred to others." Now an experience may be difficult, even impossible to describe; but that does not make it irrational or absurd.

The Christian faith, as writers such as Thomas Aquinas reminds us, does not contradict reason but transcends it. It is a principled recognition of the limits of our capacity to cope with immensity, often alluded to by Augustine of Hippo's words: "If you can comprehend it, it's not God." Our reason is unable to take in the vastness of the intellectual landscape of the divine, just as our words are unable fully to express what we encounter. In one sense, the doctrine of the Trinity is our admission that, as created, finite, fallen and flawed beings, we simply cannot fully grasp or express all that God is. We have to do the best we can and accept its limitations.

TRADITION

We now need to come back to the idea of tradition, which I introduced earlier. The English word *tradition* comes from the Latin term *traditio*, which means "handing over," "handing down" or "handing on." It is a thoroughly biblical idea. Thus we find Paul reminding his readers that he was handing on to them core teachings of the Christian faith, which he had himself received from other people (1 Corinthians 15:1-4). The term can refer to both the action of passing teachings on to others—something which Paul insists that must be done within the church—and to the body of teachings that are handed on in this manner.

The Pastoral Epistles in particular (three later New Testament letters that are especially concerned with questions of church structure and the passing on of Christian teaching— 1 Timothy, 2 Timothy, and Titus) stress the importance of guarding "the good deposit that was entrusted to you" (2 Timothy 1:14).

The New Testament also uses the notion of "tradition" in a negative sense, meaning something like "human ideas and practices which are not divinely authorized." Thus Jesus Christ was openly critical of certain human traditions within contemporary Judaism (e.g., see Matthew 15:1-6; Mark 7:13).

The importance of the idea of tradition first became obvious during the second century with the arising of the Gnostic controversy. This centered on a number of questions, including how salvation was to be achieved. (The word *Gnostic* derives from the Greek word *gnosis*, "knowledge," and refers to the movement's belief in certain secret ideas that had to be known in order to secure salvation.) Christian writers found themselves having to deal with some highly unusual and creative interpretations of the Bible. How were they to respond to these? Was every interpretation of the Bible to be regarded as of equal value?

Irenaeus of Lyons (c. 130-c. 200), one of the early church's greatest theologians, did not think so. The question of how the Bible was to be interpreted was of the greatest importance. Heretics, he argued, interpreted the Bible according to their own taste. Orthodox believers, in contrast, interpreted the Bible in ways that their apostolic authors would have approved. What had been handed down from the apostles through the church was not merely the biblical texts themselves, but a certain way of reading and understanding those texts.

Irenaeus's point was that a continuous stream of Christian teaching, life and interpretation could be traced from the time of the apostles to his own period. The church was able to point to those who had maintained the teaching of the church, and to certain public standard creeds which set out the main lines of Christian belief. Tradition was thus the guarantor of faithfulness to the original apostolic teaching, a safeguard against the innovations and misrepresentations of biblical texts on the part of the Gnostics.

But for those of us living in the twenty-first century, tradition is more than that: it is about having access to the treasure chest of two thousand years of Christian reflection on what it means to be a believer, on how best to understand and communicate the faith, and how to live out the Christian life. To use Sir Isaac Newton's famous phrase, we are able to see further because we stand on the shoulders of giants. Contemporary Western culture is dominated by an ideology of the ephemeral, based on philosophies and values that are not expected to endure more than a decade or so. To take the "great tradition" seriously is to anchor oneself to a community of reflection, to overhear their conversations and meditations, and thus to be enriched, nourished and above all given *stability*.

In chapter two we will look further at how theology enriches faith and reflect on the role of the theologian.

MERE THEOLOGY

The Landscape of Faith 2

THEOLOGY MAPS THE LANDSCAPE OF FAITH, enabling the richness of the Christian faith as a whole to be enhanced by a deeper appreciation of its various components.[1] How might some theological analysis help us in this process of appreciation?

Let's look at an example to help us explore this point. What is the significance of the Eucharist? (Christians, of course, have used a wide variety of terms to refer to this, including Mass, Holy Communion and Lord's Supper.) How can attending, taking part in or leading the Eucharist help enrich personal faith? We can easily identify four different levels of meaning within this sacrament, each of which is important theologically.

1. Recollection: Looking backward. First, the Eucharist invites Christians to look backward into the past, and recalls the saving acts of God in general, and above all, the cross and resurrection of Christ. The general principle of recollecting God's saving acts is firmly established in the Old Testament. For example, many of the psalms (such as Psalm 136) invite Israel to remember how God delivered them from Egypt and lead them into the Promised Land. The basic theme is simple: the God who acted faithfully in the past may be relied on to do the same in the present and the future.

The recollection of the past also emphasizes the continuity between the church and Israel, the New and Old Covenants. It has often been pointed out that the Eucharist can be seen (though the parallel is not exact) as the Christian equivalent of the Passover. According to the Synoptic Gospels, the Last Supper was a Passover meal, suggesting that Jesus wished his followers to make a connection between the past act of delivering Israel from Egypt, and the greater act of deliverance that was about to take place.

(2) *Anticipation: Looking forward.* Having invited Christians to look backward in remembrance, the Eucharist then points to the future, inviting Christians to anticipate what has yet to take place. This theme is deeply embedded in the New Testament. For example, Paul's account of the Eucharist makes specific reference to its anticipation of the return of Christ in the future (1 Corinthians 11:23-26): "For as often as you eat this bread and drink the cup, you proclaim the Lord's death until he comes" (NRSV). And we find the theme too in the vision of the New Jerusalem offered by the book of Revelation, which speaks of "the marriage supper of the Lamb" (Revelation 19:9 NRSV). The reference here is to Jesus Christ as the "Lamb of God, who takes away the sin of the world" (John 1:29). It is important to see the Eucharist as a present celebration of this future event. For this reason, the Second Vatican Council referred to the Eucharist as a "foretaste of the heavenly banquet." The early church writer Theodore of Mopsues-

tia (c. 350-428) wrote that the Eucharist allows us to glimpse the realities of heaven and anticipate our future presence there. We peer through the portals of the New Jerusalem and yearn to join its praise.

(3) *Affirming individual faith.* Another function of the sacraments is to affirm the present faith of individual believers. This process of affirmation takes place through the mind and imagination. The believer, who is located in the present, is able to reflect on what God has done in the past, anticipate what God will do in the future and deepen his or her faith, and trust in God as a consequence.

This understanding of the role of the Eucharist in supporting individual faith is found throughout Christian history. It became particularly significant during the sixteenth-century Reformation, as leading Protestant thinkers emphasized the importance of trusting God, even in situations of great uncertainty. For the first generation of Protestant reformers, the sacraments were God's way of providing reassurance to believers, despite their weakness and lack of trust. The sacraments represent and reinforce the gracious promises of God, using objects of the everyday world to help us grasp and cling on to the faithfulness of God.

(4) *Affirming corporate belonging.* Sacraments can be regarded as strengthening the mutual support of members of the Christian community. In a sense, this can be seen as the original meaning of the Latin word *sacramentum*—a solemn oath of obedience and commitment. For a society to have any degree of cohesion, there must be some act all can share in that both demonstrates and enhances that unity. This point was developed by Augustine of Hippo in the early fifth century. "In no religion, whether true or false, can people be held together in

association, unless they are gathered together with some common share in some visible signs or sacraments."

Theological analysis helps us to identify and explore these four different levels of meaning of the Eucharist. It allows us to see the individual trees, rather than being overwhelmed by the woods. It offers us a map, which enables us to make sense of and get more out of our pilgrimage of faith. Like a guide to a great work of art, theology points things out that we might otherwise miss, enabling us to notice, appreciate and ultimately benefit from them.

It is important to realize the potential of this theological unpacking for Christian preaching, pedagogy and spirituality. For example, let us consider the themes of "remembering" and "anticipating" in a little more detail. Both played a pivotal role in the Old Testament understanding of the significance of the exodus from Egypt. Israel is constantly reminded to remember its exile in Egypt and recall all that God has done for it since then (Psalms 135:5-14; 136:1-26). Israel looked back to its deliverance from Egypt and remembered the faithfulness of the God who had called the nation into being. It looked ahead with an eager hope to the final entry into the land which flowed with milk and honey. As Israel struggled through the wilderness, these were anchors that secured faith in times of doubt.

Again, the same themes kept the people of Israel's hopes and faith alive during the long captivity of Jerusalem in Babylon during the sixth century before Christ. The familiar words of Psalm 137 capture the sense of longing felt by the exiles for their homeland:

> By the rivers of Babylon we sat and wept
> when we remembered Zion.

The thought of returning to the homeland sustained the exiles throughout the long and harsh years of exile. It can also sustain us today. We live on earth; our homeland is in heaven. The Christian journey is thus poised between past and future, and is sustained by *memory* on the one hand and *anticipation* on the other.

So how is the theologian to share and apply such insights? How can theology serve the community of faith? Let me offer some reflections on the calling and role of the theologian, using a series of four loose categories to help us in our explorations.

A RESOURCE PERSON FOR
THE LOCAL CHRISTIAN COMMUNITY

The theologian is called to anchor the church to its rich past, to identify and apply approaches, insights and practices from the long tradition of Christian reflection on Scripture to present situations. The theologian is like the householder "who brings out of his storeroom new treasures as well as old" (Matthew 13:52). The study of theology prevents endless reinvention of the wheel on the part of those who recognize the need to engage a situation or issue, but are unaware that the church has already developed the tools needed to cope with them.

Most clergy, through no fault of their own, have little more than a superficial acquaintance with the richness of the Christian tradition. How could contemporary approaches to theological education ever allow more than a highly selective surface reading of the tradition when something approaching total immersion is really needed? The theologian, on the other hand, ought to be able to see how past insights can inform and nourish the contemporary church and help clergy to discover and apply this rich resource to their ministry.

Those of us who are theologians may wish to take this idea further and think of developing a "local theology"—a vision of the Christian faith as it is best expressed for our community. This will mean getting to know its preferred ways of speaking and thinking, and the situations it faces. We are likely to have to take into account important issues of culture, class, ethnicity and history as we frame the gospel proclamation for the people we know and serve. I explore this in greater depth in chapter six.

AN INTERPRETER OF THE CHRISTIAN
TRADITION TO THE CHURCH

How is the theologian to interpret the tradition to the church? An answer is readily to be found by looking at the approaches of those who have visited the treasure chests of the past and found jewels to enrich contemporary spirituality and church practice. Thomas Merton (1915-1968), for example, reworked some themes from the monastic writer Bernard of Clairvaux (1090-1153) to engage with the concerns of the modern church. Many in the West in the late 1960s were turning to Eastern religions for insight into spirituality. Merton saw this growing cultural interest in Zen Buddhism as a symptom of a cultural yearning for something that Christianity already possessed yet seemed to have forgotten or lost. Merton's attempts to revive and restate these traditions are regarded by many as representing a landmark in Christian spirituality.

Similarly, the English evangelical writer J. I. Packer's long study of the Puritan tradition persuaded him that though it had to be approached *critically*, this important period in Christian history had much to offer the contemporary church. Both Merton and Packer offer a theology of retrieval: we reach into the theological past in order to bring greater depth and stability to the present. Obviously these two examples are selective. There are many other treasures from the past waiting to be appreciated and applied to our present Christian concerns to help us cope with things as much as to understand them.

We do theology in company—in conversation with others who have thought about these things before us. Think, for example, of the question of suffering. Those who wrestle with this question intellectually might look to writers such as Augustine or C. S. Lewis or Richard Swinburne to help us find workable answers. There are many others who do not necessarily expect to be able to understand everything but who want to be able to deal with suffering as an existential issue. Seeking reassurance that God remains real in their lives, despite their pain and grief, they are more likely to read Martin Luther or Jürgen Moltmann, two writers who show how the suffering of Christ enables the believer to cope in times of personal crisis.

AN INTERPRETER OF THE CHRISTIAN TRADITION TO THE WORLD

The theologian is also called to interpret the Christian tradition to the world. Christian withdrawal into cosy clubs or safe places is not acceptable. We are called to be salt and light to the world—to be a redemptive, transforming and renewing presence in our communities.

The need for a Christian presence and voice in our culture has never been greater. As the recent rise of the new atheism has made clear, apologetics is of increasing importance to the church. Theology informs apologetics, enabling the apologist to have a full and firm grasp of the richness of the gospel, and hence an understanding of which of its many facets might be the most appropriate starting point or focus when faith is challenged. By refreshing our vision of God theology ensures that we constantly present faith as a dynamic, transformative reality to our culture. We speak of God, not in terms of the wooden repetition of the past, but with the excitement and passion of discovery and commitment.

A FELLOW TRAVELER WITHIN THE COMMUNITY OF FAITH

Theology is often seen as a discipline that lacks connections with the life and witness of the church. I have no doubt that this can be the case; I have no doubt that it ought not to be. To appreciate this point let us consider some of the giants of Christian theology. Athanasius of Alexandria, Augustine of Hippo and Martin Luther were all passionately committed to the life and well-being of the church, while C. S. Lewis regularly attended his local Anglican church in Headington, Oxford.

None of these theologians were outsiders, dispassionate external observers; rather they shared in the life of the church and regarded it as vital to their own mission and ministry. They saw no tension between the intellectual exploration of the Christian faith and its practical outworking in spirituality, preaching, ministry and pastoral care. The growth in the number of books with titles such as *Pastoral Care in the Classic Tradition* has alerted us to the profoundly *theological* yet simultaneously profoundly *practical* approach of these theologians, which has much to offer the church of today.

Of course, there is nothing wrong with theology being taught and studied in universities! But we have to be careful that it does not lose its rooting in worship, prayer and adoration. The great American poet and naturalist Henry David Thoreau (1817-1862) once complained that "there are nowadays *professors* of *philosophy*, but not philosophers." If we can see what he means by that, we can probably also see how to avoid becoming detached theologians. Theology is at its best and at its most authentic when it is put into practice in ministry, mission and worship.

Studying theology is like a voyage of discovery: we find spectacular new vistas opening up for us. But as we become more familiar with the great ideas, words and images of faith, there is a danger we will begin to take them for granted. Part of our theological journeying will be to keep them fresh and alive. We must try to maintain an outsider perspective, ask ourselves, What is there about these ideas and images that could transform the outlook of someone who presently knows nothing about the life of faith? Are there new ways of presenting and visualizing these themes that will help others appreciate them? The church's intellectual pilgrimage has always included exploring new ways of presenting old truths—truths which sometimes become trapped, like flies in amber, in language and imagery of long bygone days.

And that brings us to a point of no small importance. Those of us called to be theologians need to study theology with the needs of the community of faith in mind: What difference does this idea make to the way we see the world? How could I preach this idea? How does it inform pastoral care? Long ago, I took to heart these words of C. S. Lewis:

> I have come to the conclusion that if you cannot translate your own thoughts into uneducated language, then your thoughts are confused. Power to translate is the test of having really understood your own meaning.

How, for example, would we explain the term *salvation* in "uneducated language"? What stories would we tell to get the idea across? What images and analogies would we use to engage the imagination of our audience?

Each of us needs to work the angles of the rich theological heritage of faith, interpreting and applying this great tradition for our community. We will come to know its way of thinking and speaking, its concerns and aspirations, and learn to relate to it the Christian gospel using language and imagery that are transparent.

Finally, we must emphasize the link between theology and worship. Theology has done its job well when it leaves us on our knees, adoring the mystery that lies at the heart of the Christian faith. There is a sense in which worship provides a context and offers a corrective to theology.

Worship provides a *context* for theology in that it represents a vigorous reassertion of the majesty and glory of God. It reminds us of the greater reality behind the ideas and language that theology can be overconcerned with getting right. When theology becomes dull and stale, worship can rejuvenate it: worship is the fiery crucible of joy in which theology can reconnect with its true subject. In this way worship corrects inadequate conceptions of theology, especially those which treat theology simply as a set of ideas.

Yet theology can also act as a corrective to worship. Worship can too easily be seen as a purely human activity, capable of enhancement and adjustment by appropriate techniques. But true worship is not improved by whipping up the emotions or turning up the music; rather it is enhanced and authenticated by reflecting on who God is and thus naturally yearning to respond in praise and adoration. If I could borrow a phrase from John Henry Newman, it is through the devotional, spiritual, prayerful practice of Christianity that we come to have a "real apprehension" (rather than a purely "notional apprehension") of what theology is all about.

To conclude: the church is a community of vision, given its identity and mission by the gospel of Christ. Without a clear idea of its calling and purpose, the church will fade away, the custodian of cultural memories that fewer and fewer want to recall. We cannot live on memories; we can, however, live and act on the powerful and energizing vision that has been passed down through the apostles to us. Theology can help us appreciate its vitality, proclaim its excitement and live out its joy and delight in the world.

Yet the Christian faith is about far more than making sense of this world; it is about holding out the hope of something better—a new creation and the New Jerusalem. Theology does not merely help us appreciate the landscape of faith in this world. It gives us a vision of another landscape over the horizon, a new world that is yet to be born, and assures us that we shall be part of it. Mere theology is about sustaining the Christian hope for the future, not just fostering the Christian understanding in the present. Like Moses, we can climb the mountain to see over the river to the Promised Land, where one day we shall dwell. Theology helps us to see this world in its proper perspective.

Many medieval theologians stressed that there was no greater privilege or pleasure than to finally be able to behold God face to face. This privilege was reserved for heaven, when the limitations imposed on human nature by its creatureliness and sinfulness would be thrown aside. Bernard of Cluny (c. 1100-c. 1150) expressed this hope as follows—a hope which theology helps sustain, articulate and communicate:

> There God, our King and portion,
> In fullness of his grace,
> Shall we behold for ever
> And worship face to face.

THE GOSPEL AND THE TRANSFORMATION OF REALITY

George Herbert's "Elixir"

D<small>O NOT BE CONFORMED TO THIS WORLD</small>, but be transformed by the renewing of your minds" (Romans 12:2 NRSV).[1] Throughout his writings, we find Paul reaffirming the transformative power of the gospel—its capacity to change human lives, including the way we understand the world and behave within in and toward it.

The New Testament uses a wide range of images to describe this transformation, many of which suggest a change in the way we see things: our eyes are opened and a veil is removed (Acts 9:9-19; 2 Corinthians 3:13-16).[2] We are unable to see things as they actually are, unless we are helped to see. This was an important point for the British moral philosopher and novelist Iris Murdoch, who emphasized that "by opening our eyes we do not necessarily see what confronts us. . . . Our minds are continually active, fabricating an anxious, usually self-preoccupied, often falsifying *veil* which partially conceals the world."[3] This veil must be removed, our eyes must be healed, and both these are works of divine grace, not human skill or achievement. To use a way of thinking characteristic of Augustine of Hippo, divine grace "heals the eye of the heart,"[4] allowing us to see the world as it really is, rather than in a fragmented and distorted manner.

Theology is thus about *discernment*, seeing reality in a certain way and attempting to resolve its ambiguities through this interpretative framework.[5] But how are we to visualize this changed way of seeing the world? How are we to grasp it with the power of the imagination, rather than simply comprehend it with our minds? In what way does the Christian gospel so enhance our capacity to behold things that we may discern the footprints of God in the sands, the tracks of his passing in the walkways of life and his presence and power in our everyday experiences? While we should never neglect the importance of reason and understanding, we must also value the power of the human imagination as the gatekeeper of the human soul.

Theology is an activity of the imagination as much as of reason, in which we seek to transcend the boundaries of the given, pressing upward, outward and forward. Theology frames the landscape of reality in such a way that our everyday existence is set in a wider perspective. The world, formerly an absolute end in itself, now becomes a gateway to something greater.

In recent years theologians and scholars of literature have paid increasing attention to the theological richness of the poetry of George Herbert (1593-1633). There is a growing consensus that Herbert, though steeped in and informed by the tradition of the European Reformation, possessed a rare ability to transform this theology into rhetorical forms capable of captivating the imagination.[6] Underlying Herbert's poetry is an understanding of the role of words to bridge the gap between heaven and earth, between the believer and Christ.[7] Herbert's use of evocative figures of speech (tropes) allowed him to establish significant links between the secular and profane world and the core themes of the Christian faith.[8] His genius was to offer a way of expressing these themes that was powerful and imaginative compared to the learned biblical commentaries and dense tomes of systematic theology of his age.

This was an issue of no small importance to Herbert. His writings show an acute awareness of the importance of audience and the limitations placed on words as a means of communication.[9] The poem "Windows" opens with a question addressed to God:

Lord, how can man preach thy eternal word?

Yet this quickly transposes into a discussion of the limits of purely verbal forms of preaching, which risk being "waterish, bleak, and thin." To be faithful and effective, preaching must marry and merge "doctrine and life, colours and light." Herbert's poetry itself can be seen as an attempt to enact the preacher's role to be a window for divine truth, which affects real life, not simply the understanding.[10]

Herbert's collection of poems *The Temple* is widely regarded as a literary and theological treasure, and has excited much interest and comment. For example, does the arrangement of its constituent poems reflect some deeper theological or liturgical structure?[11] We shall not explore this important question here but will focus instead on what is often described as the most beautiful and meaningful of Herbert's works—"The Elixir."

The poem was initially titled "Perfection" and opened with

the following stanza, which identifies God as the point of reference for both rational and moral judgments.

> Lord teach me to refer
> All things I do to thee
> That I not only may not err
> But also pleasing be.

Herbert revised "The Elixir" extensively,[12] in response to both literary and theological concerns.[13] The first draft of the poem seems to focus on how the believer appears to God; the final draft is concerned more with how the believer acts for God.[14] Yet the most significant change concerns the choice of analogies for the transformation of vision and action that Herbert regards as an integral element of the Christian faith.

Initially, Herbert shows a clear preference for analogies drawn from the living world of nature. Yet from the third draft onward these are displaced by analogies drawn from the inorganic world of alchemy. A significant final verse is introduced, containing a controlling image that comes to dominate the poem—Christ as the fabled philosopher's stone.[15]

> This is that famous stone
> That turneth all to gold:
> For that which God doth touch and own
> Cannot for less be told.

This alchemical image is deeply significant, both from a literary and theological perspective. The classic image of the philosopher's stone makes a powerful appeal to the human longing to be able to transcend the limits of the ordinary world. Base metals could be transmuted into gold; mortality into immortality.[16] English writers of the Middle Ages and Renaissance were clearly familiar with alchemical literature and terminology, and though its leading themes were widely ridiculed in literary circles[17]—Francis Bacon, for example, expressed concern about its "credulous and superstitious traditions"[18]—the potency of the imagery made its eventual deployment in sermons and poems inevitable. The great Puritan preacher Richard Sibbes (1577-1635) spoke of the grace of God as "a blessed Alchemist," in that "where it toucheth it maketh good and religious."[19] John Donne and George Herbert were thus not alone in believing that this intoxicating imagery could be put to literary, even theological use, to yield a "true religious alchemy."[20] Donne uses several alchemical images in his poems addressed to the Countess of Bedford. Perhaps more importantly, we find the alchemical "tincture" playing a significant iconic role in his *Resurrection, Imperfect*. Christ is here portrayed as the one who transmutes the base metals of fallen, mortal human nature to his immortal and imperishable nature.

> For these three days become a mineral.
> He was all gold when He lay down, but rose
> All tincture, and doth not alone dispose
> Leaden and iron wills to good, but is
> Of power to make e'en sinful flesh like his.

Herbert's alchemical imagery offered an imaginative framework by which the transformative impact of Christ upon believers' perceptions of the world and their place within it could be expressed poetically. Where theologians and preachers of his age generally used abstract concepts to express the new attitudes that faith in Christ engendered—such as a theology of work or vocation[21]—Herbert chose to deploy words and images with the capacity to linger in the minds of the faithful and thus permanently to affect how they saw the world. Christ, the philosopher's stone, transforms, transmutes and transvalues the humble, mean life of the believer into something that is significant and valued. This theme is found at several points in Herbert's *Temple*, as in the important poem "Easter":

> Rise, heart; thy Lord is risen. Sing his praise
> > Without delays.
> Who takes thee by the hand, that thou likewise,
> > With him mayst rise.
> That, as his death calcined thee to dust,
> His life may make thee gold, and much more, just.

The poem envisions Christ as the agent of transformation from dust to gold, from ashes to precious metal.

Yet it is arguably in the later versions of Herbert's "Elixir" that we find the most sophisticated theological application of the imagery of alchemy, focusing on three core concepts: the "Philosopher's Stone" itself, a substance that was believed to have the power of transmuting base metal into gold; the "Elixir," a powder derived from this stone; and a "Tincture," produced by mixing this powder with a liquid such as water or alcohol. The alchemical literature points to a wide variety of interpretations of these notions, and they are probably best regarded as essentially fluid concepts.[22] For Herbert's purposes, each is to be regarded as an agent of transmutation and transvaluation; when brought into touch with base metals, each has the power to transform metal into gold.

So how does this bear on theology? How does Herbert's "Elixir" illuminate the ability of theology to transform our perceptions of the world and hence our actions within it? The first stanza of the poem sets the scene for the discussion that follows. Often criticized for their banality,[23] these lines emphasize the importance of "seeing" the world correctly.

Teach me, my God and King,
In all things thee to see,
And what I do in any thing,
To do it as for thee.

These opening lines contain the core themes that pervade
this poem. For Herbert the disciplined skills required to see
things as they really are must be thought of as an initial gift of
divine grace, which are subsequently honed through the
preaching and sacraments of the church. The habits of thinking underlying the mature Christian engagement with reality
are thus acquired from God, rather than from innate human
intelligence or experience. These habits of thought then lead
from reflection on the world to action within the world. All of
these themes, of course, are widely recognized to be commonplace within the Lutheran, Reformed and Anglican theological traditions known to Herbert, directly or indirectly. Herbert's genius lies not in their origination but in how they are
expressed and explored poetically.

So how does this help us reflect on the traditions and tasks
of Christian theology? Herbert's conception of the role of theology in the Christian life is to be found in the third stanza of
the "Elixir":

A man that looks on glass,
On it may stay his eye;
Or if he pleaseth, through it pass,
And then the heav'n espy.[24]

Herbert here contrasts two quite different possible modes of
engagement with a piece of glass—a "looking on" and a "passing through." There is a clear parallel with the poem "Windows," noted earlier, which explores how a human preacher,

though little more than "brittle crazy glass," may act as a window through which God may be more fully known.[25] The observer may look at the window, seeing it as an object of interest in itself. Yet there is a deeper mode of engagement, in which the observer uses the window as a gateway, a means of gaining access to a greater reality. Indeed, the window itself may become a distraction, in that the viewer focuses on the sign, rather than what is being signified.[26]

Herbert's analogy illuminates two possible ways of doing theology. The first is to look at the window itself, allowing our eye to "stay" on its physical structures and appearance. Likewise, we may study theology by considering its core ideas and their mutual relationships, by gaining a deeper understanding of the historical contexts within which they emerged, or by reflecting on how best these may be expressed or explained.

Yet Herbert's preference is clearly for a second mode of engagement: using theology as a means of envisioning a transformed reality. Theology makes possible a new way of seeing things, throwing open the shutters on a world that cannot be known, experienced or encountered through human wisdom and strength alone. Christian doctrine offers us a subject worth studying in its own right; yet its supreme importance lies in its capacity to allow us to pass through its prism and behold our world in a new way.

Having established this point, Herbert then makes a series of moves that consolidate this critical role for theology in discerning the true nature of things and the manner of habitation and action that is appropriate for believers in the world. Theology articulates and frames the transvaluation of reality, which takes place on account of Christ, turning the mundane into the epiphanic, base metals into gold. The gospel changes the realities of life through the death and resurrection of Christ.[27] Theology is not the agent of this transformation; it is, however, the agent of its disclosure.

> All may of Thee partake;
> Nothing can be so mean
> Which with his tincture (for Thy sake)
> Will not grow bright and clean.

Herbert invites us to see the world in a new light—a world that has been brightened and cleansed through Christ's suffering and death. Nothing that comes into contact with Christ can be "mean"—lowly, humble, commonplace or worthless. His theological vision discloses and describes the grand inversion of values within the new ordering of reality resulting from the gospel, in which the first become the last, the humble noble.[28]

> A servant with this clause
> Makes drudgery divine:
> Who sweeps a room as for Thy laws,
> Makes that and th' action fine.

Christ sprinkles every aspect of the believer's actions with grace, forcing us to see both the agent and action in a new light. Herbert thus links the transformation of vision with that of agency, holding that the Christian gospel enables and authorizes a specific manner of beholding both the moral agent and the moral task.

It is interesting to compare Herbert's understanding of the evangelical transformation of reality with that of C. S. Lewis. Herbert's poetry is dominated by the notion of the gospel coming into contact with humanity. "The Elixir" is unusual, in that this contact is described in somewhat impersonal and physical terms, using the controlling images of the philosopher's stone, a tincture and the elixir. All these are agents of transmutation that need to be *applied* to what is to be transformed. Unless the tincture is applied to the wound, it will not be healed. Elsewhere in the *Temple*, Herbert uses images of personal contact—for example, the image of Christ taking the believer "by the hand."[29] Herbert's imagery here is drawn from the Gospel narratives, which portray Christ as reaching out to touch individuals or taking them by the hand (Mark 1:31, 41; 5:41; 7:32; 8:23; 9:27). The gospel is an alchemy of grace, which transforms by application, as a medicine is applied to a wound by a physician.

Lewis similarly affirms the transforming capacity of the gospel. Yet the dominant imagery that Lewis deploys is that of illumination. God is like the sun, whose rays lighten the world, altering human perceptions. It would be no criticism of Lewis to suggest that he seems to be incorrigibly Platonic at this point,[30] tending to think of God as the intelligible Sun who gives light to the mind and therefore intelligibility to all that is now seen.[31]

Lewis's emphasis on the importance of "seeing" as a metaphor for human engagement with a greater reality may reflect the priority assigned to this mode of perception by many German Romantic writers:[32] his interest in the Romantic notion of *Sehnsucht* is evident at many points in his writings.

A particularly striking instance of this imagery may be found in Lewis's early sonnet "Noon's Intensity." Here, God is portrayed as a sun whose "alchemic beams turn all to gold."[33] The sonnet appears to leave open the question as to whether this illumination transmutes nature itself or merely human perceptions of nature, but it is possible to argue that Lewis's dominant idea is that of the divine metamorphosis of human vision.[34] This stands at some considerable distance from Herbert's approach, which sees the transformation of reality and of human perception as interlinked, both being dependent on the gospel as a "tincture" that heals and amends.

Much more could be said about Herbert's approach to transvaluation in the "Elixir," not least the manner in which he reworked the poem to make alchemy central to the development of its argument and imagery. The important point is that Herbert offers us a vision of theology as a lens or window through which we look to discern the transcendent in the everyday, heaven in the ordinary. There are few better starting points for the appreciation of the role of theology in the Christian life than this.

The Cross, Suffering and Theological Bewilderment

Reflections on Martin Luther and C. S. Lewis

How do we make sense of things?[1] This is one of the oldest and most basic questions of human existence. We quite naturally try to identify patterns in the rich fabric of nature to offer explanations for what happens around us, to find a deeper order of things that will help us understand our lives. This is more than a quest for truth; it is fundamentally a search for meaning and significance.[2]

Many discover that the Christian faith makes sense of life. I became a Christian at the age of eighteen while studying chemistry at Oxford University. (For the story of how I came to faith, see chapter seven.) My conversion related to my perception that Christianity offered a more comprehensive, coherent and compelling account of reality than the atheism I had embraced in my earlier teenage years. It seemed to me to possess a double rationality: Christianity made sense in itself, and it made sense of everything else as well. While fully conceding the inevitable limits of arguments from history, experience and reason, I saw these as convergent pointers to the greater reality of God. They couldn't prove the existence of God with the total certainty that some might like, but if the God of the Christian faith possessed the profundity, wonder and sheer glory that the New Testament suggested, there was no doubt that he had a deeply embedded capacity to make sense of the riddles of life.

C. S. Lewis was one of the figures who helped me most reflect on the rationality of the Christian faith. Although it is still fashionable in academic circles to question Lewis's credentials as a theological thinker, I must confess that what I found, and continue to find, in his writings makes it impossible for me to endorse that judgment.

The first part of my pilgrimage took the form of an exploration of the new intellectual landscape that the Christian faith made possible. Lewis affirmed the intellectual capaciousness of the Christian faith, arguing that it was on the one hand well-grounded, and on the other enriching and enabling. His writings illustrate the intellectual and imaginative implications of the transformation of humanity through faith, embracing the human mind as much as the heart and soul.

Lewis helped me to appreciate that embracing the Christian faith did not entail committing intellectual suicide. In no way does the gospel demand the displacement or degradation of the human mind; rather, human reason is illuminated and energized through faith so it may transcend its natural limitations. There is evidence that Lewis himself became weary of his apologetic ministry later in life, finding it draining of his own faith.[3] Yet his writings encouraged me (and many others!) to take such a "discipleship of the mind" with the greatest seriousness.

Realizing that studying Christian theology in some depth would be an essential part of my journey of faith, I moved from Oxford to Cambridge University in 1978 in order to focus on the theological writings of the early sixteenth century.

I began a detailed study of the great German Reformer Martin Luther (1483-1546). Although my theological research concentrated on understanding the development of Luther's doctrine of justification by faith, especially when set in its historical context, I devoured his early writings, whether they dealt specifically with this topic or not. In the spring of 1979, I came across Luther's "theology of the cross," which he developed over the period 1517-1521.[4] It became clear to me that the emergence of this theology was closely linked with the shaping of his distinctive theology of justification.

But I found the core ideas of the theology of the cross deeply puzzling. One of Luther's bolder statements in particular left me all at sea: "Living, even dying and being damned, make a theologian, not understanding, reading or speculating."[5] This seemed to me to verge on the nonsensical. What was theology if it was not about reading books and trying to make sense of things? Luther seemed to be pointing toward a theological trajectory that bore little relation to that I knew and valued.

As I read on, I came across other terse statements emphasising the centrality of the cross of Christ to faith. "The cross alone is our theology."[6] "The cross puts everything to the test."[7] I could certainly make some degree of sense of these. Like many young theologians, I had spent much time reflecting on "theories of the atonement" and had quite well-developed views about how best to understand the meaning of the cross.

Yet Luther's words seemed to go far beyond any such theory of the manner in which the salvation of the world was achieved.

They suggested that the cross of Christ was a key to Christian existence—to our knowledge of God and the dynamics of the Christian life. A "theology of the cross" was about seeing the cross of Christ as a lens through which we should view reality.

I found myself being bombarded with ideas that challenged both my existing understanding of faith and the role of theology in articulating that faith: we cannot grasp God fully; we are walking in the dark, rather than in the light; our grip on reality is only partial and deeply ambivalent; we are assaulted by temptation, doubt and despair. Above all, Luther stressed that the cross offers us the most secure standpoint from which to view and cope with these deep ambiguities within the natural order, human culture and our own experience. "The one who perceives the visible rearward parts of God as seen in suffering and the cross deserves to be called a theologian."[8] Luther's controlling image here is that of Moses being denied a clear and direct vision of a glorious God, and having to content himself with an indirect vision of a God disappearing into the shadows (Exodus 33:18-23). If Luther was right, any idea about theology offering us clear and precise ideas would have to be modified significantly. Where C. S. Lewis spoke of the light of the gospel illuminating reality, comparing God to an intellectual sun, Luther spoke instead of the "darkness of faith."

I wish I could say that I walked away from my engagement with Luther inspired by his theology of the cross, and that he opened a new chapter in my own theological development. But historical accuracy will not allow me to do this. While I gained a very good understanding of the historical process by which Luther had arrived at his ideas, it remained unclear to me why these were of such importance. The simple truth is that I was not ready for them.

Why not? As I look back on my own life around that time, I can identify two main reasons why this was the case. First, because my early vision of the Christian faith was rather cerebral and academic; while I had come to appreciate the rational resilience of Christianity, I had thus far failed to fathom its relational and existential depths.

Second, I was still quite deeply influenced by an idea that can be traced back to Descartes and that played a leading role in the eighteenth-century Enlightenment—that our experience of reality can be expressed using "clear and distinct" language.[9] Reality was not "fuzzy" or ambiguous; any view of reality would thus be able to give a "clear and distinct" account of things. It was a view which allowed little place for complexity, ambivalence or doubt. To me, these were the symptoms of sloppy, inexact or muddled thinking.

At this early stage in my development, I therefore regarded it as self-evident that theology aimed for conceptual precision—a precision, I may add, which I believed I had found (though in different ways) in both Karl Barth's *Church Dogmatics* and Thomas Aquinas's *Summa Theologiae*. I did not find it in Luther. I judged him to be at fault in this matter and thus welcomed the attempts of later Lutheran writers to systematize his ideas, iron out his conceptual wrinkles and bring methodological order to his often impulsive writings.

The seeds of doubt about my early approach to theology were sown during the years 1980-1983, when I served as a curate in the parish church of St. Leonard in Wollaton, a suburb of Nottingham. Nothing demonstrates the futility of a purely academic approach to theology so powerfully as parish ministry. Working with my congregation forced me to confront the shallowness of my understanding of theology at that time: it proved to be cerebral, dry and unrelated to the harsh realities of human experience; unable to cope with the fuzziness of doubt and the messiness of sin. Where, I wondered, could I find a theology that connected with the big questions of living, dying, doubt and despair that I was encountering? With the corrupting influence of power and the destructive effects of the human quest for status and influence? With the damaging impact of low self-esteem? With the limitations of human nature to grasp and comprehend things?

I began to realize that Luther's theology of the cross offers a way of placing suffering within a greater framework. For Luther the issue is not primarily how can we explain suffering—which is there, whether we like it or not—but how can we cope with it,[10] and how can God use it to enable us to grow into stronger, better people?[11]

A similar approach emerges in the writings of Simone Weil (1909-1943). Weil, who discovered Christianity relatively late in her short life, was fully aware of the brutalizing impact of evil. She doubted whether it was ever possible to offer a rational explanation for its presence or a means of evading it. Yet for Weil, "The extreme greatness of Christianity lies in the fact that it does not seek a supernatural remedy for suffering but a supernatural use for it."[12] Divine wisdom is known through human misery *(malheur)*, rather than through pleasure. Indeed, "all pleasure-seeking is the search for an artificial paradise,"[13] which discloses "nothing except the experience that it is vain." Only the contemplation of our "limitations and our misery" raises us up to a higher plane.

Luther points to the tensions that arise when reason leads us in one direction and our emotions in another. We find our faith being battered, because it has no firm foundation, no point of attachment to a deeper reality which is able to weather the storms of life. For Luther, the cross of Christ is a stabilizing and integrating reality, the rock upon which our house of faith may be built. The cross is a definitive disclosure of the despair that results when reason and emotions pull in separate directions; when God is *believed* to be present, but not *experienced* as present. By seeing the cross as a paradigm of the "darkness of faith," we can cope with the ambiguities and contradictions of our experience of the world, which often threaten to lead us away from God as much as to disclose him.

Luther's theology of the cross poses a significant challenge to theologically inflated accounts of reality that hold that we can see further and more clearly than our situation permits.[14] This resonates with a theme that runs through much postmodern writing, namely, that we cannot hope to achieve "totalization"—that is, to gain a comprehensive grasp of the deep structures of reality.[15] *Any* theory—whether religious, scientific or secular—has a limited capacity to represent the totality of things[16] and will thus find itself in tension with what is experienced of the world. That's just the way things are. The problems begin when we think it ought to be otherwise and so reject the worldview because it cannot accommodate the totality of experience. We must settle for the best fit, not the perfect fit.

This is why Luther insists on a perpetual return to the foot of the cross, the source of true theology. In the physical brutality, the aesthetic ugliness, the conceptual fuzziness and the spiritual messiness of the crucifixion of Christ, we find a reassertion and reassurance of the hidden presence and activity of God in this puzzling, disturbing and often overwhelming world.[17] Just as God spoke to Job from the whirlwind, so Luther insists that God speaks to us from the cross to proclaim his presence. He is very present in this scene of hopelessness and helplessness, even if we find it difficult to articulate this using the neat categories of our theology.

Luther's theology of the cross recognizes the essential darkness in which faith finds itself. It invites us to envision the Christian believer contemplating a darkened, misty landscape, where little can be seen for certain. Yet even in this dark and obscure world, there are things that we can hold onto—above all, the trustworthiness of the Christ who took upon himself suffering, dereliction and death. We may trust him and entrust ourselves to him. The cross, like Mount Sinai, may be enfolded by clouds and darkness. Yet God remains present in this darkness, transcending both our capacity to discern him and our willingness to trust him. Luther's point is that we do not walk alone but in the presence of the one who was crucified for us, and who will never abandon us, having already journeyed through the valley of the shadow of death.

The "Word of the Cross," according to Luther, does not destroy or even totally dispel this spiritual darkness; nevertheless, it reveals it for what it truly is and provides enough light for us to make our way within it, one step at a time. Indeed, there are times when Luther seems to think of Christ as a candle, projecting a flickering circle of light, allowing us to find our bearings and our way. Beyond that candle, all is dark and unknown. Yet we cannot make the candle burn brighter. We must trust the one who holds it, and leads us in the gloom. "The light shines in the darkness, and the darkness did not overcome it" (John 1:5 NRSV).

When I left Wollaton to return to Oxford in the summer of 1983, I had finally grasped why Luther's theology of the cross was so important. I had come to appreciate the weakness and vulnerability of any theology that failed to secure a synergy of reason and feeling. Spending time with the bereaved on the eve of funerals forced me to realize the emotional and relational shallowness of what were otherwise well-argued theological ideas.

I continued to read Lewis, finding him an ongoing source of inspiration and enlightenment in many areas. But there were shadowlands, areas of his thought which now left me dissatisfied. His *Problem of Pain* (1940) seemed to me to be rationally illuminating yet existentially deficient. Somehow, it failed to penetrate to the real issues underlying human suffering, appearing to suggest that the problem of pain could be sorted out by a good dose of rational reflection on the problem. I began to have doubts about its pastoral value and spiritual insight. It was fine for university discussion groups; it was not much use when I was trying to say something helpful to someone who had been bereaved.

I was not the only one to come to such a conclusion. In 1961 a short work by N. W. Clerk appeared with the title *A Grief Observed*. The volume consists of the painful and brutally honest reflections of a man whose wife has died, slowly and in pain, from cancer. It includes a vivid depiction of his own reaction to her death, as well as some more theological reflections on the goodness of God. How can what has happened make sense, if God is good and loving?

Clerk realizes that his rational, cerebral faith has taken something of a battering. The ideas that had once proved anchors to his life have turned out to be inadequate in the face of catastrophe: "Nothing will shake a man—or at any rate a man like me—out of his merely verbal thinking and his merely notional beliefs. He has to be knocked silly before he comes to his

senses. Only torture will bring out the truth. Only under torture does he discover himself." The slow death of Clerk's wife
does not lead him to unbelief; it does, however, reveal the pre-
carious nature of a faith based only on ideas and disconnected
from the harsh realities of life and the emotional responses
these engender.

Now "N. W. Clerk" was a pseudonym for none other than
C. S. Lewis himself, noted for celebrating the rationality of
faith that he now believed to be inadequate to sustain him. In
The Problem of Pain, Lewis had argued that belief in God was
consistent with the existence of suffering in the world. His neat
theological slogans, dispersed throughout the book, describing
pain as God's "megaphone to rouse a deaf world,"[18] seem more
than a little trite, simplistic and above all *inadequate* in relation
to the suffering and death of his wife, Joy. To its critics Lewis's
approach in *The Problem of Pain* reduces evil and suffering to
abstract ideas, which require to be fitted into the jigsaw puzzle
of faith. To read *A Grief Observed* is to realize how a rational
faith can fall to pieces when it is confronted with suffering as a
personal reality, rather than as a mild theoretical disturbance.
Previously Lewis's theology had engaged with the surface of
human life, not its depths. And Lewis, we now know, recognized this.

> Where is God? Go to him when your need is desperate, when
> all other help is vain, and what do you find? A door slammed
> in your face, and a sound of bolting and double-bolting on the
> inside. After that, silence.[19]

Lewis made it clear that Joy's death served to crush all that
was self-confidently rationalist in his faith. It is little wonder
that his authentic and moving account of the impact of bereave-
ment has secured such a wide readership, given its accurate de-

scription of the emotional turmoil that results from a loved one's death. But the work is also significant for exposing the vulnerability and fragility of a rational faith that is rooted only in the mind. While Lewis undoubtedly recovered his faith after he lost his wife, *A Grief Observed* suggests that the cool, rational approach he once set out in *The Problem of Pain* has been abandoned. For example, Lewis discloses his belief that God has taught him to love Joy truly by taking her painfully from him, thus helping him to see that because their love had achieved its earthly limit, it was ready for its heavenly fulfillment.

Lewis's readers, whether critics or friends, have noted such shifts in thought and pondered their significance. John Beversluis's assessment of the changes evident in *A Grief Observed* emphasizes Lewis's realization of the existential inadequacy of his earlier views.

> *A Grief Observed* is a harrowing book not just because it deals with suffering, death, and a tottering faith, but because it reveals that Lewis's faith was rediscovered at the enormous cost of leaving unanswered and unanswerable the very questions he had all along insisted must be answered, the very questions that had proven fatal to his earlier faith.[20]

Beversluis is generally thought to overstate his case at this point; it is, however, very difficult to avoid coming to some such conclusion on the basis of a fair reading of *A Grief Observed*, especially if it is set alongside the corresponding passages of *The Problem of Pain*.[21]

The lesson that I learned from reading this moving and disturbing book is that a theology that is untested against the harsh experience of the world will always be prone to doubt and despair. Lewis's *cri de coeur* helped me appreciate what Luther was getting at. As Luther himself pointed out, experience

is ultimately what makes a real theologian.[22] Luther's theology
of the cross is perhaps best seen as a *critical* theology—one
which demands that we recognize the limitations under which
faith exists in this world. No conceptual matrix, religious or
secular, can fully cope with the immensity and complexity of
our experience. Life is indeed a mystery, something that cannot be contained within a constraining theoretical cage.

This need not—indeed, I would suggest that it *must* not—
cause us to abandon the joyful exuberance of Lewis's delight in
the capacity of the Christian faith to make sense of things.
Luther forces a correction of Lewis, not his rejection. Lewis's
emphasis on the sense-making capacity of faith can perhaps
too easily be misunderstood to mean that the Christian sun illuminates every aspect of the landscape so that no shadows remain. Luther reminds us that many aspects of that landscape
remain shrouded in darkness, and that many find themselves
called to walk in those shadowlands. Lewis is right: theology
gives us a lens through which we can interpret the world, making sense of its ordering and its enigmas. Luther is also right:
theology enables us to journey through darkness and despair.
Its lens may sometimes yield a picture that appears quite out of
focus, but not being able to view a picture clearly does not mean
there is no picture to see.

For all their differences, Lewis and Luther both believed
that we dwell in a world of shadows, which will one day give
way to the brilliance and clarity of heaven. For Lewis these
"shadowlands" are a reflection of the eternal world, whose light
seeks to pierce, illuminate and perfect our own. For Luther the
shadows are those of suffering and the apparent absence of
God within the world, which are brought into focus and seen
in their proper context through the cross of Christ. The Christ

who was crucified is the one who is with us until the end of the age (Matthew 28:20). Both Lewis and Luther were totally persuaded of the penultimacy of the present—in other words, that what we now know and experience is not the last word. That is spoken by God, a reassurance of both his presence and power: "Behold, I make all things new" (Revelation 21:5 RSV)

5

THE THEATER OF
THE GLORY OF GOD

A Christian View of Nature

FEW QUESTIONS HAVE SO INTRIGUED HUMANITY as that of the meaning of the universe.[1] The sight of a star-studded night sky can make us feel quite overwhelmed. Are these silent points of light harbingers of a more significant world than that we know? Or are they simply symbols of the vastness of space and the brevity and pointlessness of human existence?

Recently, traditional questions such as these have been supplemented by others. A growing realization of the fragility of our environment has led many to call for the development of a new attitude toward the natural world. If we are not careful, we could destroy our habitat and hence eventually ourselves: humanity could be the first species to have brought about its own extinction.

The way in which we view the domain of nature is thus obviously important. The Christian way of looking at nature faces challenges from its rivals. On one side, there has been a resurgence of paganism in the West in recent decades.[2] In its new forms, paganism represents a wide range of beliefs and practices: some forms are reappropriations of pre-Christian ideas (such as Druidism), others are better understood as postmodern constructions, reflecting a growing cultural interest in nature and spirituality.[3] Yet underlying most, if not all, is a strong sense of nature as a sacred entity, capable of disclosing its secret wisdom to those who are able to discern its deeper levels of meaning.

At the opposite end of the spectrum, another range of worldviews denies that there is any spiritual or transcendent dimension to nature. In a famous lecture of 1917, the German sociologist Max Weber spoke of the "disenchantment of the world."[4] Nature was not mysterious, sacred or "special"; it was something that could be explained and mastered by science and technology. More recently, the new atheism has vigorously asserted nature as a self-referencing entity, devoid of any deeper significance.[5]

There is no consensus within contemporary Western culture on this matter, no shared interpretation of the identity and status of the natural world. We are told that we are free to interpret as we will, and act on those interpretations.

Yet this does not prevent us from evaluating the merits of the neopagan and new atheist approaches. Postmodern writers such as Stanley Fish have emphasized the growth of "interpretive communities," each committed to its own distinctive reading of reality and its justification.[6] The church can see itself as a distinct "interpretive community," sustained by its own narrative and identified by its language, images and values. The power of the Christian interpretative community to capture the imagination of our culture will rest to no small extent on its imaginative rendering of the natural world, and on the way it defends and communicates its ideas.

Can the Christian faith offer a richer, deeper account of the natural world than its pagan or atheist rivals? The importance of the question is obvious. Both the credibility and utility of the Christian faith can legitimately be called into question if it fails to offer a better account of reality than its rivals.

Christian theology offers a distinct angle of gaze, a way of seeing things which both discloses the true identity of nature and mandates certain ways of behaving toward and within it. Theology enables us to see the fullness of reality, the world as it really is or could be. For contrary to what most thinkers of the Enlightenment believed, nature is not an autonomous, self-defined entity; rather, it is something that is always interpreted, whether consciously or unconsciously, from a theoretical standpoint.[7] The term *nature* does not designate an objective reality that requires interpretation. It is already an interpreted entity. As the great British philosopher of science William Whewell (1794-1866) once remarked, there is "a mask of theory over the whole face of nature."[8] The term *nature* thus really denotes a variety of ways human observers choose to see, interpret and inhabit the empirical world.

Christians see the natural world through a theological prism. In the eighteenth century many Christians chose to interpret nature through a lens that was deist, rather than trinitarian. God was seen as the creator of nature, whose involvement with the natural realm ceased thereafter. This encouraged the emergence of a functional atheism, in that God was, to all intents and purposes, thought of as being absent from the world.[9] Yet during the twentieth century, through the influence of theologians such as Karl Barth and Karl Rahner, there has been a rediscovery of the coherence and explanatory power of a specifically trinitarian vision of God. But perhaps we should allow that immensely gifted amateur theologian Dorothy L. Sayers to reflect on the importance of this development in her own characteristic way:

> The Christian affirmation is . . . that the Trinitarian structure which can be shown to exist in the mind of man and in all his works is, in fact, the integral structure of the universe, and corresponds, not by pictorial imagery but by a necessary uniformity of substance, with the nature of God.[10]

So what difference does this make to the way we see nature? Perhaps the most obvious is that the natural world is God's created possession, entrusted to humanity. The Christian understanding of the created order immediately negates any notion that humanity is the originator or possessor of the natural world, entitled to exploit it for its own ends. Nature has been entrusted to humanity, who is to be thought of as its steward, not its master. It is not ours, so that we may do with it as we please. We may indeed bear the "image of God" (Genesis 1:27), but this is a mark of responsibility, not privilege.[11] To bear God's image is to be accountable to God for our behavior, not to be exempt from divine scrutiny or accountability. This insight does not solve the problem of how we deal with our environmental crisis, but it does provide an essential framework within which such reflection and action may take place. The way we see things shapes how we behave toward them.

Yet further reflection leads to other insights. If God created the natural world, does it not bear the divine imprint? Is not one of the implications of a trinitarian doctrine of creation that the natural world displays in some sense the marks of its Creator? This insight is famously stated in the opening words of Psalm 19:

> The heavens are telling the glory of God;
> and the firmament proclaims his handiwork. (NRSV)

Israel already knew about its God, and did not need to look at the natural world for proof of God's existence. Yet it saw God's glory reflected in the creation. To use John Calvin's phrase, the natural world is to be recognized as the "theater of the glory of God." God's glory is stamped on the world by the act of creation; this is supplemented by the mighty acts by which God chose to redeem the world, which take place within this same theater of nature.[12] As Bonaventure of Bagnoregio (1221-1274) argued, the many features of nature can be discerned as "shadows, echoes and pictures" of God its Creator, which "are set before us in order that we might know God."[13]

While this deeper, more satisfying engagement with the natural realm allows us to appreciate its beauty and rationality, it does raise an obvious question: what of the moral and aesthetic ambiguity of nature? Is not nature characterized by ugliness as much as beauty? By violence, destruction and pain, as much as by goodness? How can this aesthetic and moral variegation within nature be accommodated theoretically?

A particularly distinctive aspect of a trinitarian reading of nature is the notion of the "economy of salvation," traditionally attributed to Irenaeus of Lyons in the second century.[14] Irenaeus uses this framework to set out a panoramic vision that encompasses the entire breadth of history, from creation to consummation. God created the world "good"; it has now defected from this primal state and is to be thought of as fallen, sinful or damaged. What might be the relevance of this theological framework for our engagement with nature?

One obvious point is that a fallen humanity here reflects on a fallen natural world.[15] Neither observer nor observed are exempt from the damage of sin. This can be developed further with reference to the present status of nature within the "economy of salvation." Nature remains God's creation but is now profoundly ambiguous, signaling both its divine origins and its present distress.

This tension is evident within the New Testament. For example, at several points Paul makes an appeal to the creation as the basis of knowledge of God. Yet while Paul clearly holds that God can be known through the creation (Romans 1), at other points he qualifies this by referring to the "groaning" of the creation (Romans 8).[16] The created order is to be seen as in transition, suspended between its original creation and final re-creation.

Engaging nature using the trinitarian framework of the economy of salvation allows the Christian interpreter of nature to accommodate the moral and aesthetic ambivalence of nature. How can the existence of a good God be inferred from such ambivalence? Or reconciled with it? When all is said and done, there are really only two options at our disposal: turn a blind eye to those aspects of nature that cause us moral or aesthetic discomfort, or develop a theological framework that allows us to affirm its primordial goodness of nature while also accounting for evil. The first approach, in addition to being intellectually disreputable, causes considerable psychological discomfort, giving rise to a potentially destructive "cognitive dissonance" between theory and observation. We are thus left with only one viable way of handling the issue—developing a framework which allows this moral ambiguity to be observed, honored and interpreted.

Such a framework is provided by the Christian faith's vision of God. It affirms that God created all things good and that they will finally be restored to goodness. Yet at present, good and evil coexist in the world, as wheat and weeds grow together in the same field (Matthew 13:24-30). This trinitarian framework allows us to locate good and evil, ugliness and beauty within the context of the theological trajectory of creation, fall, incarnation, redemption and consummation.

To explore this further, let us consider a passage from the final volume of John Ruskin's *Modern Painters* (1860), in which he reflects on a landscape in the Scottish Highlands.[17] Ruskin, one of the most influential cultural figures of the Victorian age, insists that God has given us "two sides" of nature and intends us to see them both. To make this point, Ruskin points to an unnamed "zealous" Scottish clergyman who was determined to see the landscape as a pure and simple witness to the "goodness of God." Nature is described in terms of "nothing but sunshine, and fresh breezes, and bleating lambs, and clean tartans, and all kinds of pleasantness."

Yet Ruskin dismisses this as inept. The zealous clergyman has chosen to see what he wishes to see, not see what is actually there. For Ruskin, "to see clearly" lies at the heart of poetry, prophecy and religion.[18] How can nature be sunlit without there being shadows? Ruskin offers an alternative viewing of a Highland landscape, stressing its moral and aesthetic ambivalence:

> It is a little valley of soft turf, enclosed in its narrow oval by jutting rocks and broad flakes of nodding fern. From one side of it to the other winds, serpentine, a clear brown stream, drooping into quicker ripple as it reaches the end of the oval field, and then, first islanding a purple and white rock with an amber pool, it dashes away into a narrow fall of foam under a

thicket of mountain-ash and alder. The autumn sun, low but clear, shines on the scarlet ash-berries and on the golden birch-leaves, which, fallen here and there, when the breeze has not caught them, rest quiet in the crannies of the purple rock.

Up to this point, Ruskin echoes the somewhat one-sided sentiments of the Scottish parson. Yet the shadows, he now insists, must be seen. Ruskin's mood alters, as he describes the less attractive aspects of the scene. Death and decay are present in this paradise.

Beside the rock, in the hollow under the thicket, the carcass of a ewe, drowned in the last flood, lies nearly bare to the bone, its white ribs protruding through the skin, raven-torn; and the rags of its wool still flickering from the branches that first stayed it as the stream swept it down. . . . At the turn of the brook, I see a man fishing, with a boy and a dog—a pictur-esque and pretty group enough certainly, if they had not been there all day starving. I know them, and I know the dog's ribs also, which are nearly as bare as the dead ewe's; and the child's wasted shoulders, cutting his old tartan jacket through, so sharp are they.

Ruskin thus points to a shadowy side to nature, which cannot be denied or softened by even the most zealous Romantic imagination. Yet this is the real nature that Christian theology must address—a harsh empirical reality, not some idealized and sanitized fiction.

A trinitarian perspective enables us to see the natural world as decayed and ambivalent—as something that is morally and aesthetically variegated, whose goodness and beauty are often opaque and hidden, yet are nevertheless irradiated with the hope of transformation. Christian theology is the elixir, the philosopher's stone, which turns the mundane into the epiphanic, the world of nature into the realm of God's creation. Like a lens bringing a vast landscape into sharp focus or a map helping us grasp the features of the terrain around us, Christian doctrine offers a new way of understanding, imagining and behaving. It invites us to see the natural order, and ourselves within it, in a special way—a way that might be hinted at but cannot be confirmed by the natural order itself. Above all, it allows us to avoid the fatal fundamental error that is so often the foundation or consequence of a natural theology—namely, that divine revelation is essentially reduced to the supreme awareness of an order already present in creation.

This leads us to consider a further question that arises from the Christian engagement with nature. Does nature prove the existence of God? William Paley's famous *Natural Theology* (1802) set out to demonstrate the existence of God from the evidences of design in the natural world. (I discuss Paley's work in greater detail in chapter eight.) More recently, writers such as the philosopher William Lane Craig have argued that the existence of a Creator God can be deduced from reflection on the natural world.[19] An alternative approach, however, is to appeal to the notion of "empirical fit." How well does the mental map of the Christian faith fit with what is actually observed in the world?

This approach is found in the writings of William Whewell, noted earlier, who believed the best demonstration of the existence of God lay in "showing how admirably every advance in our knowledge of the universe harmonizes with the belief of a most wise and good God."[20] The argument that Whewell puts forward is that the observation of reality is consonant with the Christian vision of God, *which is believed to be true on other grounds.* In other words, nature does not prove God's existence, yet the existence of God may be held to be the best explanation of what is actually observed.

A more recent exponent of this approach is the physicist turned theologian John Polkinghorne, who argues for "consonance" between our observations of the world and the Christian tradition.[21] Polkinghorne suggests that the capacity of mathematics to mirror the deep structures of reality is highly significant: "There is a congruence between our minds and the universe, between the rationality experienced within and the rationality observed without."[22] For Polkinghorne this can be explained in terms of the created correspondence between the human mind and the natural order. I have elsewhere developed a similar way of thinking, noting the "resonance" between the Christian vision of things and what is actually observed.[23]

This approach does not demand that the observation of nature can *prove* the existence of God through necessary inference. Rather, it is argued that the vision of nature that is mandated and affirmed by the Christian vision of things is found to offer a highly satisfactory degree of consonance with what is actually observed. Christian theology offers, from its own distinctive point of view, a map of reality that, though not exhaustive, is found to correspond to the observed features of nature. The map corresponds to the landscape; the theory to the observation. Christian theology makes possible a way of seeing things that is capable of accommodating the totality of human experience and rendering it intelligible through its conceptual schemes. Christian theology offers us a mental map, a schema, that is able to explain much of what is observed in nature.

Where some have argued that the existence and at least some of the characteristics of God can be deduced from the natural world, Polkinghorne and I argue for a more modest and realistic approach, based on the idea of resonance or "empirical fit" between the Christian worldview and what is actually observed. The Christian faith, grounded in divine self-revelation, illuminates and interprets the natural world; the "Book of Scripture" enables a closer and more fruitful reading of the "Book of Nature." The capacity of the Christian vision of reality to illuminate and explain what is observed, while important in its own right, can also be seen as a confirmation of its reliability as a theory. This does not prove the existence of God; it does, however, point to the ability of Christianity to map the terrain of our universe.

Yet there is another aspect to the Christian engagement with nature that forms a fitting conclusion to this chapter. Christianity regards nature as a limiting horizon to the unaided human gaze, which nevertheless possesses a created capacity, when rightly interpreted, to point beyond itself to the divine. The philosopher and novelist Iris Murdoch (1919-1999) used the term *imagination* to refer to a capacity to see beyond the empirical in order to discern deeper truths about the world. This, she argues, is to be contrasted with "strict" or "scientific" thinking, which focuses on what is merely observed. An imaginative engagement with the world builds on the surface reading of things, taking the form of "a type of reflection on people, events, etc., which builds detail, adds colour, conjures up possibilities in ways which go beyond what could be said to be strictly factual."[24]

Murdoch's point here is that the imagination supplements what reason observes, thus disclosing a richer vision of reality. Her argument may falter at points; its potential outcomes, however, are important. To be limited to an empirical account of nature fails to disclose its (or our!) meaning, value or agency—

the great questions that any "theory of life" has to address.[25] Yet the Christian faith is also able to offer an approach to nature that is grounded in its empirical reality but transcends the empirical.[26] It offers us theoretical spectacles which allow us to behold things in such a way that we are able to rise above the limits of the observable and move into the richer realm of discerned meaning and value. In doing so, it does not descend into fantasy but makes warranted assertions that are grounded in its deep and rich trinitarian vision of God. The natural world thus becomes God's creation, bearing the subtle imprint of its Maker. We see not only the observable reality of the world but its deeper value and true significance. Neither value nor significance, it must be emphasized, are empirical notions, things that we can see around us. They must be discerned and then superimposed on an empirical reading of the world.

This point is developed in a short poem by the German Romantic writer Joseph von Eichendorff (1788-1857):

> In all things a song lies sleeping,
> That keeps dreaming to be heard,
> And the world will rise up singing,
> If you find the magic word.[27]

Eichendorff's point is that there is a hidden meaning to the natural world, and we need to find the key that will unlock its secrets: the "magic word" *(Zauberwort)* is widely interpreted as pointing to poetic vision, rather than scientific analysis, as enabling an authentic experience of nature. Such a key is provided by the Christian faith. Nature is an "open secret"—yet its true meaning requires special interpretation.

Unless the Christian church can offer a vision of the natural world which transcends those of its rivals in today's marketplace of ideas, it cannot hope to retain the interest of contemporary culture. Sadly, we live in an age when too many see nature simply in the cold and abstract terms of scientific analysis. But historians have long recognized that the Christian view of creation played a major role in the emergence of modern science, by stressing the ordered and rational structures of the natural world. The Christian faith also allows us to see further and deeper, to appreciate that nature is studded with signs, radiant with reminders and emblazoned with symbols of God, our Creator and Redeemer.

6

THE TAPESTRY OF FAITH

Theology and Apologetics

ONE OF MY MORE ENJOYABLE and rewarding profes-
sional responsibilities is teaching a course on the great changes
in thinking about ecclesiology—the doctrine of the church—
that have taken place since the Second World War.[1] Traditional ecclesiologies tended to see the identity and function of
the church primarily in terms of teaching, worship, pastoral
care and social engagement. This rather static idea of the
church as "chaplain" to a specific nation, community or interest group was gradually displaced by understandings that emphasized the importance of outreach to society, and argued
that this is an integral element of the church's identity.[2] It is
perhaps significant that this aspect was particularly stressed
by theologians such as Stephen Neill (1900-1984) and Lesslie
Newbigin (1909-1998), both of whom served as bishops in
India. Faced with the challenges of Christian life and witness
in a non-Christian culture, Neill and Newbigin were concerned that the church should recover a sense of the vital part

it has to play in the mission of God to the world.[3]

In an increasingly secular West we might now take such insights as self-evidently true. Yet the predominance of "chaplaincy" models of church in the West until relatively recently has impoverished our understanding of the critical impact of mission on Christian theology and theology on Christian mission. The German Lutheran theologian Martin Kähler (1835-1912) is today remembered especially for his short volume *The So-called Historical Jesus and the Historic, Biblical Christ.* Yet many would argue that his best work is a neglected essay published in 1908 on whether mission is an indispensable aspect of Christianity. Kähler argued that mission became the "mother of theology" in the early church.[4] The first theologians "wrote within the context of an 'emergency situation' of a church which, because of its missionary encounter with the world, was forced to theologize."[5] Far from being something the church undertook from a position of leisure or power, theology was integral to the church's task as it reached out into new cultural situations.

APOLOGETICS AND EVANGELISM

Today, the outreach of the church in the West could be loosely organized under two headings: apologetics (which we looked at briefly in chapter two) and evangelism. Briefly, apologetics can be seen as an attempt to demonstrate that the Christian faith is able to provide meaningful answers to the "ultimate questions," such as, Where is God in the suffering of the world? or Is faith in God reasonable? Evangelism, on the other hand, moves beyond this concern with clearing the ground for faith in Christ and invites people to respond to the gospel. Apologetics aims to secure consent; evangelism aims to secure commitment.

David Bosch's influential definition of evangelism makes this point well:

> Evangelism is the proclamation of salvation in Christ to those who do not believe in him, calling them to repentance and conversion, announcing forgiveness of sins, and inviting them to become living members of Christ's earthly community and to begin a life of service to others in the power of the Holy Spirit.[6]

While the dividing line between apologetics and evangelism is fuzzy, the distinction between them is helpful. Apologetics is conversational; evangelism is invitational.[7]

THEOLOGY AND APOLOGETICS

Where does theology come into apologetics? I want to suggest that theology has two significant contributions to make to responsible Christian apologetics. First, it insists that we set apologetics in its proper context; second, it allows us to appreciate the richness of the gospel and identify what the best "point of contact" might be for the gospel in relation to a given audience—in other words, to form an apologetic vision. We shall consider each of these points separately.

Setting apologetics in context. First, a proper understanding of Christian theology gives us a mental map which allows us to locate the resources and tasks of apologetics. Apologetics is often presented simply as a technique for winning arguments. Avery Dulles is one of many influential writers to express concern about such theologically deficient approaches, noting their "neglect of grace, of prayer, and of the life-giving power of the Word of God."[8] Yet a right understanding of apologetics, resting on a secure theological foundation, insists that God is involved in the apologetic enterprise. It is unthinkable to dissociate the grace of

God from the undertaking of commending God. To think of apologetics in terms solely of human techniques and arguments is to run the risk of lapsing into some form of Pelagianism,[9] which neglects, perhaps even denies, God's presence, power and persuasion in the task of apologetics.

Furthermore, the apologetic task cannot be limited to developing arguments. In some way we must realize that apologetics involves enabling people to glimpse something of the glory and beauty of God. It is these, not slick arguments, that will ultimately convert and hold people. True apologetics engages not only the mind but also the heart and the imagination, and we impoverish the gospel if we neglect the impact it has on all of our God-given faculties. The great eighteenth-century American Puritan theologian Jonathan Edwards (1703-1758) remains one of the most significant critics of a purely rationalist approach. He believed rational argument has a valuable and important place in Christian apologetics, but it is not the sole and perhaps not even the chief resource of the apologist.

> Great use may be made of external arguments, they are not to be neglected, but highly prized and valued; for they may be greatly serviceable to awaken unbelievers, and bring them to serious consideration, and to confirm the faith of true saints . . . [Yet] there is no spiritual conviction of the judgment, but what arises from an apprehension of the spiritual beauty and glory of divine things.[10]

Arguments do not convert. They may remove obstacles to conversion and support the faith of believers, but in and of themselves they do not possess the capacity to transform humanity. For Edwards true conversion rests on an encounter with a glorious and gracious God. This insight is liberating in that it reaffirms that apologetics is not about developing manipulative human techniques but about recognizing and coming to rely on the grace and glory of God. However, it also raises the question of how we can appreciate the wonder and joy of the gospel—a point to which we now turn.

Appreciating the richness of the gospel. This brings us to the second theological dimension of apologetics—the need to appreciate the richness of the Christian gospel and reflect on how best to communicate this to a given audience. The task of the apologist is to know both gospel and audience, and be able to identify the best means of translating the great themes of Christian faith into a specific cultural vernacular. Or to put it another way, good apologetics rests on two essential responsibilities:

1. *Theological reflection* on the gospel, to ensure that we have appreciated it in all its fullness;

2. *Cultural reflection* on the audience, *initially* so we may select those aspects of the gospel that will resonate most strongly, and *subsequently* to consider how best to articulate these aspects.

Reflecting theologically on the gospel. Theological reflection on the gospel proclamation affirms its unity, while at the same time revealing its complexity. We earlier considered the idea of the Christian faith as a tapestry, in which a series of threads are woven together to yield a richer, more complex whole. Appreciation of the "big picture" has always been a fundamental theme of Christian apologetics, and many find such grand narratives deeply attractive, not least because they enable us to find our place within them and to make sense of things.

Let us dwell for a moment on some of the individual components that make up the overall pattern of our "tapestry." Several threads in this fabric of faith concern the Christian understanding of human nature. These threads are both *ontological*, speaking of the identity of human nature, and *teleological*, its ultimate goal and purpose. We have been created to relate to God and fail to achieve our true goal until we do so. God has planted eternity in our hearts (Ecclesiastes 3:11), so that our heart's true desire lies with God. This is famously summed up in the well-known theological prayer of Augustine of Hippo: "You have made us for yourself, and our heart is restless until it finds its rest in you."[11] A theological understanding of human identity may lead to the uncovering of secret longings and help people to consciously articulate their hopes and fears, or name their heart's true desire. Augustine, Blaise Pascal and C. S. Lewis all believed that the Christian faith itself brought human nature into sharp focus, thus allowing them to identify apologetic approaches tailored to the realities of our situation.[12]

Another thread in this tapestry of the faith is the notion that the cross and resurrection of Christ free us from the fear of death.[13] Christ has been raised from the dead, and those who have faith will one day share in that resurrection and be with him forever. Socrates may have shown us how to die with dignity; Christ enables us to die in hope. This great message will speak to most people, in different ways, but it has a special relevance and resonance to those who wake up in the middle of the night, frightened by the thought of dying.

Or consider another thread, the great theme of the cross: forgiveness. Through the death of Christ, real forgiveness of our real sins is possible. Redemption is indeed a precious and costly matter, something that we must mull over in our minds as we ponder the privileges of faith. Yet this aspect of the cross will also speak with particular force and power to a particular group of people: those who feel that they can hardly continue living on account of the guilt that burdens them.

They can be assured that those sins can be forgiven and their guilt taken away.

Theological analysis leads to an enhanced appreciation of the richness and glory of the gospel, and hence to the identification of apologetic possibilities. It inspires us and equips us for the apologetic task. On the one hand, it excites our minds and imaginations, and generates a passionate desire to share the richness of our faith; on the other, it helps us work out how best to do this. Once we have conducted a theological analysis of the gospel and identified which of its many aspects to draw out, we may thus move on to the second core element of the apologetic task.

Reflecting culturally on ways of proclaiming the gospel. Apologetics is audience specific. It deals with particular concerns arising from the experiences of real people and uses arguments, illustrations and ways of speaking appropriate to local situations.[14] To illustrate this point, we may consider some of the classic speeches in the Acts of the apostles, each of which show a clear and principled statement or defense of the gospel in terms adapted to the cultural situation of their respective audiences.

- An excellent example of an apologetic address aimed at a Jewish audience is provided by Peter's Pentecost sermon (Acts 2:14-36).[15] Peter cites an authority that carries weight with those he is addressing—the Old Testament. He demonstrates that Jesus meets the specific expectations of Israel by appealing to prophetic passages, while using language and terminology his audience would readily have accepted and understood. Note in particular his reference to Jesus as "Lord and Christ." No explanation is offered, nor was it necessary.

- Peter's sermon on the Day of Pentecost contrasts sharply with Paul's apologetic address at Athens—the famous "Areopagus

speech" (Acts 17). This Greek audience had no knowledge
of the Old Testament, nor would they see it as carrying any
cultural weight. Paul thus opens his address to the Athenians
with a gradual introduction of the theme of the living God,
allowing the religious and philosophical curiosity of the
Athenians to shape the contours of his theological exposition.[16] The "sense of divinity" present in each individual is
here used as an apologetic device. What the Greeks held to
be unknown, possibly unknowable, Paul proclaims to have
been revealed through the resurrection of Christ.

• Finally, we may note an apologetic address to a Roman audience. The most important speeches in Acts to deal with
  Christianity in the eyes of the Roman authorities are found
  in chapters 24–26. Recent studies have stressed the way these
  speeches conform to patterns which were well known in the
  legal proceedings of the period.[17] In his point-by-point refu-
  tation of his accusers in Acts 24:10-21, Paul follows the "rules
  of engagement" laid down by Roman legal custom. Paul thus
  argues along lines that carried cultural weight and intellectual plausibility in the minds of his listeners. He knew how
  to present evidence most effectively to his audience, following the legal conventions they were familiar with.

These early apologetic speeches and sermons point to the
need to relate the same gospel to different audiences, who will
have different ways of thinking, different core cultural values
and beliefs, different criteria of evidence and rationality, and
different aspirations. The challenge we face is to correlate the
gospel with these cultural realities, faithfully and effectively.
How do we present evidence? What authorities should we cite
in securing a cultural hearing? What are the points of contact
between the gospel and our culture? In all these things, an-

swers can be found through a close reading of the apologetic addresses of the Acts of the apostles.

The reasonableness of faith. This cultural analysis of the audience must also extend to include reflection on what individuals and communities might find compelling, attractive or persuasive about the Christian faith. It is always difficult to defend ideas that seem countercultural, going against the grain of dominant cultural ways of thinking. Yet it needs to be done. We cannot assume that people will automatically appreciate the truth and relevance of ideas that are being culturally sidelined in many parts of Western culture. We need to help people to see the power and potential of the Christian faith.

We can learn something here from the apologetic approach of C. S. Lewis. Commenting on Lewis's approach, the Oxford theologian and New Testament scholar Austin Farrer suggested that his success was partly due to his ability to offer "a positive exhibition of the force of Christian ideas, morally, imaginatively, and rationally." If Christian faith cannot make possible a vision of reality that exceeds those offered by its secular and religious alternatives in its truth, beauty and goodness, Christianity cannot hope to prosper. Yet it possesses all these characteristics; our task as apologists is to enable the rational, imaginative and moral vitality of the Christian vision of reality to be seen and appreciated within our culture.

We are thus called upon to demonstrate and embody—not to create or invent—the truth, beauty and goodness of faith.[18] Yet while Farrer acknowledged the importance of all these dimensions of faith, he was particularly concerned to point out how demonstrating the reasonableness of faith was important for its cultural acceptance.

Though argument does not create conviction, the lack of it destroys belief. What seems to be proved may not be embraced; but what no one shows the ability to defend is quickly abandoned. Rational argument does not create belief, but it maintains a climate in which belief may flourish.[19]

To demonstrate the reasonableness of faith does not mean proving every article of faith. Rather, it means showing that there are good grounds for believing that these are trustworthy and reliable.[20] It also means showing that the Christian faith makes sense of what we observe and experience.

This point was emphasised by French philosopher and social activist Simone Weil, who discovered that faith in God illuminates reality in a far better way than its secular alternatives.

> If I light an electric torch at night out of doors I don't judge its power by looking at the bulb, but by seeing how many objects it lights up. The brightness of a source of light is appreciated by the illumination it projects upon non-luminous objects. The value of a religious or, more generally, a spiritual way of life is appreciated by the amount of illumination thrown upon the things of this world.[21]

The ability of a theory to illuminate reality and bring it into sharp focus is itself an important measure of its reliability. We see here a core theme of Christian apologetics: there are good reasons for believing that Christianity is true, and one of them is the extent to which it makes sense of what we see around us and within us.

We must, however, avoid thinking that our task is simply to win arguments, or to set out the rational credentials of faith. The Enlightenment has had an enduring impact on Western culture, especially in generating demands for proofs for beliefs. As a result, Christian apologetics has often been presented simply in terms of developing effective arguments, designed to persuade people that the Christian faith is true. Yet this can all too easily end up making Christianity seem like a list of dull facts and abstract ideas. There are three especially troubling difficulties with this approach.

First, it is not well-grounded in the Christian Bible. A rationalist notion of "truth" has here displaced the biblical idea of truth as a relational concept. Truth, especially for the Old Testament, primarily designates reliability and trustworthiness. The apologetic issue is that God is a secure base, a place of safety on which to build the life of faith. The "true God" is not merely a God who exists but a God who may be relied upon.

Second, the appeal of the Christian faith cannot be limited to the rationality of its beliefs. As the writings of C. S. Lewis indicate, Christianity also makes a powerful appeal to the imagination. As a young man, Lewis found himself yearning for a world of passion, beauty and meaning that he had come to believe did not and could not exist. "Nearly all that I loved I believed to be imaginary; nearly all that I believed to be real I thought grim and meaningless."[22] His imagination told him there was a better world; his reason told him that this was nonsense. He therefore believed that he had no option other than to confront the bleakness of a senseless world and his pointless existence.

In the end Lewis discovered the rational force of the Christian faith. Yet his attraction to the gospel was based on his perception that it offered meaning, rather than propositional correctness. As Lewis later commented, "reason is the natural organ of truth; but imagination is the organ of meaning."[23] Others locate the appeal of the Christian faith in the beauty of its worship, its capacity to engage the human emotions or its ethical outcomes.

And third, this rationalist approach is deeply embedded in a modernist worldview. Yet throughout most of Western culture today, this has been displaced by postmodernity, which inverts many of modernity's core beliefs. An appeal to the intrinsic rationality of faith works well in a modern context, but in other contexts an apologetic approach based on argument and reasoning will fail to connect up with cultural aspirations and prejudices. Postmodernity's interest in narratives, rather than arguments, offers new possibilities for biblically based apologetics, given the predominance of narrative forms within Scripture.[24]

It remains of vital importance to assert and affirm the reasonableness of faith, without limiting faith to what reason can prove with certainty. The really big questions of life go far beyond what human reason is able to demonstrate. These are questions such as: Who am I? Do I really matter? Why am I here? Can I make a difference?[25] Neither science nor human reason can answer these questions. Yet unless they are answered, life is potentially meaningless. As apologists we need to show that the Christian faith offers answers to life's big questions, which are reasonable on the one hand and work in practice on the other. There are times when it is just as important to show that Christianity is *real* as it is to show that it is *true*.

CONCLUSION

Theological analysis is only one aspect of good apologetics; it requires supplementation by analysis of cultural criteria of acceptability and attractiveness. There can be no doubt of the importance of both tasks. Theological reflection helps us grasp the richness, splendor and joy of the gospel; cultural discernment enables us to anchor this proclamation in the everyday life of our audiences. Both are an integral part of the mission of the church. The urgent needs of our situation must not be allowed to lead to a shallow apologetic pragmatism, or still worse, to a loss of apologetic nerve. Now, more than ever, we need to proclaim and display the tapestry of faith, so that both its pattern and its rich component threads can be recognized and appreciated.

PART TWO

ENGAGING WITH OUR CULTURE

THE NATURAL SCIENCES

Friends or Foes of Faith?

THE RELATIONSHIP OF THE CHRISTIAN FAITH and the natural sciences has long been a concern of mine.[1] The main issue we shall explore in this chapter is whether the natural sciences are locked in mortal combat with religion. This viewpoint has long been discredited by serious scholarship, and I regard it as indefensible historically or philosophically. However, it continues to find an afterlife in the writings of the new atheists, especially those of Richard Dawkins, as we shall see.[2]

My love affair with the natural sciences began when I was nine or ten. The night sky seemed to me overwhelmingly beautiful, and I longed to explore it further. I ransacked my school library for books on astronomy and even managed to build myself a small telescope so I could observe the moons of Jupiter. Around the same time, a great-uncle who had headed up the pathology department at the Royal Victoria Hospital, Belfast, gave me an old German microscope, which allowed me to investigate another new world—one of intricate detail. It still sits on my study desk, a reminder of the power of nature to enthrall, intrigue and provoke questions.

One particular question troubled me greatly: What was life all about? What was its meaning? While in my teens, I had absorbed an uncritical atheism from writers such as Bertrand Russell. Atheism was, I believed, the appropriate worldview for a scientifically informed person such as myself. The natural sciences had expanded to inhabit the intellectual space once occupied by the derelict idea of God. There was no need to propose, let alone take seriously, such an outmoded idea. God was a baleful relic of the past, revealed as a delusion by scientific advance.

So as I reflected on the scope and power of the sciences, I gradually came to the view that there was no meaning to life. I was the accidental byproduct of blind cosmic forces, the inhabitant of a universe in which one could speak only of direction, not of purpose. It was not a particularly appealing idea, but I found solace in the thought that its bleakness and austerity were certain indications of its truth. It was so unattractive that it just had to be right. I must confess to a certain degree of smugness at this point, a sense of intellectual superiority over those who found solace and satisfaction in their belief in God.

Yet questions remained. As I continued to examine the night sky, I found its silence disturbing. I used to enjoy looking through my small telescope at M31, the famous nebula in the constellation of Andromeda, which is bright enough to be seen by the naked eye. But I knew it was so distant that the light now leaving the nebula would take two million years to reach earth, by which time, obviously, I would have died. I began to reflect on the troubling brevity of human life. What was the point of anything? The poet Alfred, Lord Tennyson's lines from

"The Brook" seemed to sum up the human situation:

> For men may come and men may go,
> But I go on for ever.

However, I remained obstinately convinced that the metaphysical severity and existential dreariness of this position were confirmations of its truth. Nobody would believe this morose and morbid stuff because it was attractive; therefore they believed it because it was right. It was axiomatic that science demanded atheism, and I was willing to be led wherever science took me.

I continued working at mathematics, physics and chemistry, eventually winning a scholarship to Oxford University to study chemistry (where the sciences, interestingly, were still referred to as "natural philosophy"). At that stage, most people gained admission to Oxford in the seventh term of the sixth form. I heard that I had won a scholarship to Oxford in December 1970, but was not due to begin student life until October 1971. What to do in between? Most of my friends left school in order to travel or earn some money. I decided to stay on and use the time to learn German and Russian, both of which would be useful for my scientific studies. Having specialized in the physical sciences, I was also aware of the need to deepen my knowledge of biology. I settled down to an extended period of reading and reflection.

After a month or so, having exhausted the works on biology in the school science library, I came across a rather small section I had never noticed before. It was labeled "The History and Philosophy of Science" and was heavy with dust. I had little time for this sort of stuff, tending to regard it as uninformed criticism of the certainties and simplicities of the natural sciences by those who felt threatened by them. Philosophy, like theology, was just pointless speculation about issues that could be solved through a few decent experiments, was it not?

By the time I had finished reading the school's somewhat meager holdings in this field, I realized that far from being half-witted obscurantists who placed unnecessary obstacles in the relentless place of scientific advance, writers such as Karl Popper and Thomas Kuhn were asking all the right questions about the reliability and limits of scientific knowledge, even if their answers seemed to require much further discussion. These were questions I had not faced thus far, relating to the under-determination of theory by data, radical theory change in the history of science, the difficulties in devising a "crucial experiment" and the enormously complex issues associated with determining what was the "best explanation" of a given set of observations. These issues crowded in on me. They muddied what I had taken to be the clear, still and above all *simple* waters of scientific truth.

Things were rather more complicated than I had realized. My eyes had been opened, and I knew there was no going back to the childlike attitude to the sciences I had once enjoyed. Secretly I wished I could recover the beauty and innocence of that stage: indeed, I think part of me dearly wished that I had never come across "The History and Philosophy of Science" section at all! But I had tasted forbidden fruit and had to enter further into this secret garden of knowledge. Though I did not come to believe in God because of the new insights I gained, an important barrier to faith was removed—namely, the idea that we must be able to prove our beliefs with certainty.

October 1971 finally arrived and I began my university studies. Up until that point I had assumed that when science could not answer a question, there was no answer to be had. I now began to see that there might be limits to the scientific method and that vast expanses of intellectual, aesthetic and moral territory might lie beyond its compass. If science could not explore them, then other ways of gaining access to these realms would have to be found. And, having been forced to abandon what I now realized to have been a somewhat naive scientific positivism, it became clear to me that a whole series of questions I had dismissed as meaningless or pointless had to be examined again—including the God question.

I began to comprehend that the natural world is conceptually malleable. Nature can be interpreted, without any loss of intellectual integrity, in a number of different ways. Some "read" or "interpret" nature in an atheist way. Others "read" it in a deistic way, seeing it as pointing to a Creator divinity who is no longer involved in its affairs. (God winds up the clock, then leaves it to work on its own.) Others take a more specifically Christian view, believing in a God who both creates and sustains the universe. One can be a "real" scientist *with* or *without* being committed to any specific religious, spiritual or antireligious view of the world.

This is the view of most scientists I speak to today, including many who self-define as atheists. Unlike their more dogmatic atheist colleagues, they can understand perfectly well why some of their colleagues adopt a Christian view of the world. They may not agree with that approach, but they are prepared to respect it. For example, Stephen Jay Gould, whose sad death from cancer in 2002 robbed Harvard University of one of its most stimulating teachers and a popular scientific readership of one of its most accessible writers, was absolutely clear on this point. The natural sciences—including evolutionary theory—

were consistent with both atheism and conventional religious belief.[3] Unless half his scientific colleagues were total fools—a presumption that Gould rightly dismissed as nonsense which- ever half it were applied to—there could be no other responsi- ble way of making sense of the varied responses to reality on the part of such intelligent, informed people.

When I realized that a love of science allowed much greater freedom of interpretation of reality than I had been led to be- lieve, I began to explore alternative ways of looking at things. I had been severely critical of Christianity but had never ex- tended that same critical evaluation to atheism, tending to as- sume that it was self-evidently correct. During October and November 1971, it became obvious to me that the intellectual case for atheism was rather less substantial than I had sup- posed: indeed my doubts about its intellectual foundations be- gan to coalesce into a realization that atheism was actually a belief system, whereas I had somewhat naively assumed that it was a factual statement about reality. At the same time, I was discovering that Christianity was far more robust intellectually than I had ever imagined. I had some major rethinking to do, and by the end of November my decision was made: I turned my back on one faith and embraced another.

It did not take me long to begin to appreciate the intellectual capaciousness of the Christian faith. Not merely was it ration- ally and evidentially well-grounded, it was also enabling and enriching. Here was a lens that enabled reality to be brought into sharp focus; a source of intellectual illumination that al- lowed me to see in the world of nature details and interconnec- tions I would otherwise have missed altogether. The Christian faith both made sense in itself and of things as a whole.

In September 1974 I joined the research group of Professor

Sir George Radda, based in Oxford University's department of biochemistry. Radda was then developing a series of physical methods for investigating complex biological systems, including magnetic resonance approaches. My particular interest was developing innovative physical methods for examining the behavior of biological membranes, which eventually extended to include techniques as different as the use of fluorescent probes and antimatter decay to study temperature-dependent transitions in biological systems.

But my real interest was shifting elsewhere. I never lost my fascination with the natural world. I just found something else rising, initially to rival it and then to complement it. What I had once assumed to be the open warfare of science and religion increasingly seemed to me to represent a critical yet constructive synergy, with immense potential for intellectual enrichment. How, I found myself wondering, might the working methods and assumptions of the natural sciences be used to develop an intellectually robust Christian theology? And how could I properly explore this possibility?

I decided the best way forward was to cease active scientific research and become a theologian. I was determined, however, to be a theologian who was up to date in his reading of the scientific literature, especially in the field of evolutionary biology, and who actively sought to relate science and faith. I had no time for the "God of the Gaps" approach, which attempted to defend the existence of God by an appeal to gaps in scientific explanation. While an undergraduate at Wadham College, I had come to know and respect Charles Coulson (1910-1974), Oxford University's first professor of theoretical chemistry, who was a vigorous critic of this approach. For Coulson reality as a whole demanded explanation. "Either God is in the whole of Nature, with no gaps, or He's not there at all."[4]

As I reflected on the cognitive implications of the Christian faith, I came to see that there is a high degree of intellectual resonance between the Christian vision of reality and what we actually observe. This led me to become interested in the field of natural theology, which I do not interpret as an attempt to deduce the existence of God from a cold, detached observation of nature, but rather as the enterprise of seeing nature from the standpoint of faith, emphasizing the importance of belief in God in explaining the "big picture." What I have in mind here are the overall patterns of ordering discerned within the universe—those things that are either too big or too odd for science to explain.[5]

For example, I came to appreciate that the explicability of nature was itself astonishing and required an explanation in its own right. I was not alone here. Albert Einstein pointed out back in 1936 that "the eternal mystery of the world is its comprehensibility." The *intelligibility* of the natural world, demonstrated by the natural sciences, raises the question as to why there is such a fundamental resonance between human minds and the structures of the universe. Why should we be able to make sense of the world at such a deep level? It seems to confer no obvious evolutionary advantage! But it is surely one of the most exciting things about the Christian faith that it creates intellectual space for the natural sciences by articulating a vision of an ordered reality that is open to study by a human mind shaped in the "image of God."

A further example of "big" and "odd" things about the universe that seem to demand an explanation are what are now widely described as "anthropic phenomena."[6] The language of "fine-tuning" has increasingly been found appropriate to express the idea that from the moment of its inception, the universe appears to have possessed certain qualities conducive, at this point in cosmic history, to the production of intelligent life on earth that is capable of reflecting on the implications of its existence. Nature's fundamental constants turn out to possess reassuringly life-friendly values. For example, the existence of carbon-based life on earth depends on a delicate balance of physical and cosmological forces and parameters which are such that were any one of these quantities to be slightly altered, the balance would be destroyed and life would not exist. While these phenomena do not represent a proof of the existence of a Creator God, they are clearly consistent with the view of God encountered and practiced within the Christian faith. The observation of anthropic phenomena thus resonates with the core themes of the Christian vision of reality.

Yet it is impossible to reflect on the natural sciences and faith without being aware of some of the challenges that appear to arise. In the remainder of this chapter, I would like to consider briefly five of the more common concerns.

THE ALLEGED "WARFARE" OF SCIENCE AND RELIGION

Richard Dawkins persistently portrays science and religion as being at war with each other. This leads to the conclusion that scientists who believe in God are nothing more than collaborators or traitors. Sadly, these views remain widespread in popular scientific culture, which still suggests that the church imprisoned and tortured Galileo for his views on the heliocentric model of the solar system, that medieval Christians thought the earth was flat and that the church fought against painless childbirth in the aftermath of the discovery of the anesthetic properties of chloroform.

Historians of science have long since discredited this "warfare" model of the relation of science and religion, as well as most of the alleged evidence in its support,[7] pointing out that the truth is far more complex than this simplistic stereotype suggests. Yet it seems to be integral to Dawkins's defense of his atheism in *The God Delusion*. Surely it's time for the new atheism to move on and catch up with current scholarship.

A FAILURE TO UNDERSTAND THE CHRISTIAN NOTION OF "GOD"

Scientific atheists often challenge Christians to prove the existence of God, as if Christians understand God to be an object within the world—such as an additional moon orbiting the planet Mars, a new species of newt or an invisible unicorn. Perhaps they think Christians imagine God to be like an Olympian deity, sitting on the top of Mount Olympus, waiting patiently to be discovered. Of course, for the Christian, God is not an "entity" alongside the other entities in the world but rather the source, ground and explanation of all that exists. God is the creator of all things, not a member of this class of things.

One of the more puzzling features of Dawkins's new atheism is his apparently unquestioned assumption that the theist's inventory of the universe simply includes one extra (and totally unnecessary) item that is absent from an atheist's list. This universal inventory must be open to verification by scientific methods. And as the existence of this God cannot be scientifically proved, it is to be dismissed as having vanishingly small probability. Dawkins does not believe in such a God. But then, neither do I.

The philosopher Ludwig Wittgenstein is noted for his emphasis that words have multiple meanings and significations. What a word means needs to be determined by the way it is used. Dawkins understands one thing by the word *God*, and I understand something quite different. The new atheism conducts its polemic against a notion of God that bears little relation to that of Christianity. Christians will not find their faith shaken by evidence or arguments that make assumptions they do not share and consider to be completely wrong. The atheist "critique" of Christianity at this point amounts to little more than a circular argument concerning the internal consistence of atheism, rather than a considered engagement with what Christians believe about God.

THE SMUGGLING OF METAPHYSICS INTO SCIENCE

When properly and legitimately applied, the scientific method is religiously neutral—neither supportive nor critical of religious beliefs. This means that scientific atheists have to spin science in certain ways in order to maintain their core dogma that science disproves religion. And since the scientific method clearly does not entail atheism, those who wish to use science in defense of atheism are obliged to smuggle in a series of nonempirical metaphysical ideas to their accounts of science and hope that nobody notices this intellectual sleight of hand.

Let us explore this point by looking at the superb recent study *The Music of Life* (2006), written by the noted Oxford systems biologist Denis Noble, who developed the first mathematical model of the workings of the human heart.[8] Noble analyzes a passage from one of Dawkins's best-known books, *The Selfish Gene* (1976), setting out the gene-centered approach to evolutionary biology, which was then gaining the ascendancy in evolutionary biology.

> [Genes] swarm in huge colonies, safe inside gigantic lumber-
> ing robots, sealed off from the outside world, communicating
> with it by tortuous indirect routes, manipulating it by remote
> control. They are in you and me; they created us, body and
> mind; and their preservation is the ultimate rationale for our
> existence.[9]

Note how Dawkins represents genes as active agents, in control
of their own destiny and ours.

So what in this passage can be proved from observation, and
what is metaphysical speculation? Noble notes that empirically
verified facts are restricted to the short statement that genes
"are in you and me." The rest is speculative. Noble then playfully rewrites Dawkins's prose, smuggling in a totally different
set of metaphysical assumptions.

> [Genes] are trapped in huge colonies, locked inside highly in-
> telligent beings, moulded by the outside world, communicat-
> ing with it by complex processes, through which, blindly, as if
> by magic, function emerges. They are in you and me; we are
> the system that allows their code to be read; and their preser-
> vation is totally dependent on the joy that we experience in
> reproducing ourselves. We are the ultimate rationale for their
> existence.[10]

On this reading, humans are in control of the situation. We are
active; genes are passive. Dawkins's position has been inverted.

So what in Noble's discussion is scientific? As before, the
only thing that can be evidentially confirmed is that genes "are
in you and me." The rest is speculative and lies beyond empirical investigation. Dawkins and Noble see things in completely
different ways. They both cannot be right. Both smuggle in a
series of quite different metaphysical assumptions. Yet their
statements are "empirically equivalent." In other words, they

both have equally good grounding in observation and experimental evidence. So which is right? How could we decide which is to be preferred on scientific grounds? As Noble observes, "no-one seems to be able to think of an experiment that would detect an empirical difference between them." The real problem in the field of science and religion has to do with the smuggling in of atheist metaphysical assumptions, which the sciences themselves neither demand nor legitimate.

SCIENCE AND RELIGION EXIST IN EXPLANATORY COMPETITION

The new atheism takes a dogmatically positivist view of science, holding that it explains (or has the potential to explain) everything, including matters traditionally regarded as lying within the religious realm. Science and religion offer competing explanations. One day, science will triumph and religious explanations will fade away. There cannot be multiple explanations of the same things, and only the scientific explanation can be valid, claim the new atheists.

Yet this is a very nineteenth-century way of arguing, resting on a failure to think critically about the nature of scientific explanation. Neuroscientist Max Bennett and philosopher Peter Hacker recently explored the "science explains everything" outlook that Dawkins and others espouse, and found it seriously wanting.[11] For example, scientific theories cannot be said to "explain the world"—only to explain the *phenomena* which are observed within the world. Furthermore, Bennett and Hacker argue that scientific theories do not and are not intended to describe and explain "everything about the world"— such as its purpose. Law, economics and sociology are examples of disciplines that engage with domain-specific phenomena without in any way having to regard themselves as somehow being inferior to or dependent on the natural sciences.

The real issue has to do with levels of explanation. We live in a complex, multilayered universe. Each level has to be included in our analysis. Physics, chemistry, biology and psychology—to note only four sciences—engage with different levels of reality and offer explanations appropriate to that level. But they are not individually exhaustive. A comprehensive explanation must bring together these different levels of explanation, in that (to give an obvious example) the physical explanation of an electron is not in competition with its chemical counterpart. My Oxford colleague John Lennox, who is a mathematician and philosopher of science, uses a neat illustration to make this point. Imagine a cake being subjected to scientific analysis, leading to an exhaustive discussion of its chemical composition and the physical forces which hold it together. Does this tell us that the cake was baked to celebrate a birthday? And is this inconsistent with the scientific analysis? Of course not.

We see here the important scientific principle of different levels of explanation, which supplement each other. This principle can easily be explored from everyday life. Consider a performance of your favorite piece of music. This can be described scientifically in terms of patterns of vibrations. Yet this perfectly valid explanation requires supplementation if is to account for the full significance of the phenomenon of music and its impact on us. Similarly, there is far more to a great painting than an analysis of its chemical components or the physical arrangement of its elements. Scientific and religious explanations can thus supplement each other. The problems start when scientists get religious or theologians scientific. For example, "creationism" is widely regarded as an example of a religious movement claiming scientific traction.

At a very simple level, we could apply this approach as follows. A scientific description of the world describes how it arose from an initial cosmological event (the fiery singularity of the big bang), which led, over a long period of time, to the formation of stars and planets, creating conditions favorable to the origination and evolution of living creatures. No reference is made, or needs to be made, to God. The Christian will speak of God bringing the world into existence and directing it toward its intended outcomes. For some, this process involves direct divine action; for others, it involves God creating and working through natural forces to achieve those goals. Yet each of these accounts supplements, rather than contradicts, the other.

BELIEF IN GOD IS A DELUSION CAUSED BY "MEMES"

Richard Dawkins first introduced the idea of the "meme" back in 1976. Toward the end of his *Selfish Gene*, he argued that there was a basic analogy between biological and cultural evolution: both involve a replicator. In the case of biological evolution, this replicator is the gene; in the case of cultural evolution it is a hypothesised entity, which Dawkins called a "meme." For Dawkins the idea of God is perhaps the supreme example of such a meme. People do not believe in God because they have given long and careful thought to the matter; they do so because they have been infected by a powerful meme, which has somehow leaped into their brains.

Yet has anyone actually seen these things, whether leaping from brain to brain or just hanging out? The real debate, it must be noted, has nothing to do with religion. It's about whether the meme is a viable scientific hypothesis, when (to mention the most obvious problems) there is no clear operational definition of a meme, no testable model for how memes influence culture and why standard selection models are not adequate, a general tendency to ignore the sophisticated social science models of information transfer already in place and a high degree of circularity in the explanation of the power of memes.

More recently in *The God Delusion* (2006), Dawkins sets out the idea of memes as if it were established scientific orthodoxy, making no mention of the inconvenient fact that the mainstream scientific community views it as a decidedly flaky idea, best relegated to the margins. The "meme" is presented as if it were an actually existing entity, with huge potential to explain the origins of religion. Dawkins is even able to develop an advanced vocabulary based on his own convictions, of words such as *memeplex*. Daniel Dennett also makes extensive use of the idea in his new atheist manifesto, *Breaking the Spell* (2006). It is fascinating that the intellectual case for new atheism depends so heavily on the idea of the meme. Yet it is a deeply flawed idea, with decidedly awkward consequences for this supposedly "scientific" approach to atheism.

To further illustrate the difficulties of this approach, we may consider Dawkins's characteristically bold statement: "memes can sometimes display very high fidelity."[12] This is a creedal statement posing as a statement of scientific fact. What Dawkins is doing is to restate an observation in his own theoretical language, which is not spoken elsewhere within the scientific community. The *observation* is that ideas can be passed from one individual, group or generation to another; Dawkins's *theoretical interpretation* of this observation—which is here presented simply as fact—involves attributing fidelity to what most regard as being a nonexistent entity. We see here an example of what most of its critics regard as the greatest failing of memetics: its "achievements" are limited to simply *redescribing* a host of phenomena in memetic terms.

Furthermore, neither ideas nor cultural artifacts can conceivably be said to be or to contain a self-assembly code. They are not "replicators," as required by the accounts of cultural transmission and development offered by Dawkins and Dennett.[13] Indeed, since there is no compelling scientific evidence for these entities, some have playfully—though not without good reason—concluded that there might even be a meme for believing in memes.

One telling indication of the failure of the meme to garner academic support can be seen in the history of the on-line *Journal of Memetics*, launched in 1997, arguably at the zenith of the cultural plausibility of the meme. The journal folded in 2005. Why? The answer can be found in a devastating critique of the notion of the meme, published in the final issue of this ill-fated journal.[14] Dr. Bruce Edmonds made two fundamental criticisms of the notion of memetics, which undermined its claims to plausibility in the scientific community.

1. The underlying reason why memetics has failed is that it "has not provided any extra explanatory or predictive power beyond that available without the gene-meme analogy." In other words, it has not provided any "added value" in terms of providing *new* understanding of phenomena.

2. The study of memetics has been characterized by "theoretical discussion of extreme abstraction and over ambition." Edmonds singles out for special criticism unrealistic and overambitious attempts, often developed in advance of evidence, "to 'explain' some immensely complex phenomena such as religion." Yet for many of its more fanatical advocates, this is pre-

cisely the point of memetics—to explain away belief in God.

Edmonds ends his incisive dismissal of the meme with its obituary: Memetics "has been a short-lived fad whose effect has been to obscure more than it has been to enlighten. I am afraid that memetics, as an identifiable discipline, will not be widely missed."

The importance of this observation will be obvious. As we noted earlier, two of the leading works of the new atheism make an appeal to the meme an integral part of their scientific case for arguing that belief in God can be explained away (most scientists would prefer to say "reductively explained"). Yet the notion of the meme turns out to be highly speculative and is significantly underdetermined by the evidence. It remains to be seen what the long-term implications of this excessive reliance on such a "a short-lived fad" (Edmonds) will be for atheist apologetics.

CONCLUSION

It is important that the Christian church engages our scientific culture positively yet critically. The scientific method, when properly applied, is no enemy of faith. The problems begin when enthusiastic atheists start smuggling in their own presuppositions, hoping nobody will notice, or when enthusiastic Christians start believing that science challenges core beliefs or essential ways of reading the Bible and circle their wagons defensively. The reality is rather different and much more interesting. The Christian faith offers us a robust intellectual vantage point, which makes sense of the historical origins and the explanatory successes of the natural sciences. Far from being a challenge to faith, the sciences—if used rightly and wisely— might even become a gateway to discovering the glory of God.

Religious and Scientific Faith

The Case of Charles Darwin's Origin of Species

THE YEAR 2009 MARKED BOTH the 200th anniversary of the birth of Charles Darwin, and the 150th anniversary of the publication of his landmark work *The Origin of Species*.[1] In this chapter I shall consider the complex yet fascinating legacy of Charles Darwin for both science and religion. In particular, I shall explore the understanding of the scientific method which we find in Darwin's core work and offer some reflections on its relevance for belief in God. This may seem a curious, even provocative, thing to do, but I hope that the points of convergence and illumination will gradually become clear.

It is impossible to read Darwin without being impressed by his deep commitment to finding the truth through observation and developing the "best explanation" of what he observed. Yet it is perhaps the style, as much as the contents, of *The Origin of*

Species that merits close attention. Darwin's graciousness and generosity have often been noted, as has his concern to correct himself where necessary. He is in many ways a role model for the natural scientist, not least in remaining as close to the observational evidence as possible and avoiding flights of metaphysical speculation.

It is intriguing that the theme of the role of faith in, and in relation to, science is so evident in the various editions of *The Origin of Species*.[2] Some may wonder, since science proves its beliefs, how this can possibly be justified. Indeed, William K. Clifford's influential essay *The Ethics of Belief* (1877) argues that "it is wrong always, everywhere, and for anyone, to believe anything upon insufficient evidence."[3] This is, he writes, not simply an intellectual responsibility; it is a fundamentally *moral* duty. Nobody should be allowed to believe something that is argumentatively or evidentially underdetermined. If Clifford's account of the scientific method were to be applied to Darwin's *Origin of Species*, we should have to reject Darwin's work as unscientific and even unethical.

The inadequacies of Clifford's approach are the subject of the famous essay "The Will to Believe" (1897), in which the Harvard psychologist William James (1842-1910) argued that human beings find themselves in a position where they have to choose between intellectual options which are, in James's words, "forced, living, and momentous."[4] We all, James argues, need what he terms "working hypotheses" to make sense of our experience of the world. These working hypotheses often lie beyond total proof, yet are accepted and acted upon because they are found to offer reliable and satisfying standpoints from which to engage the real world. For James faith is a particular form of belief, which is pervasive in everyday life: "Faith means belief in something concerning which doubt is still theoretically possible." This leads James to declare that "faith is synonymous with working hypothesis." Although sometimes accused of lending intellectual weight to what is merely wishful thinking, James would have defended himself against such a charge. Gerald E. Myers, who wrote a study of the psychologist James, observed: "He always advocated a faith sensitive to reason, experimental in nature, and therefore susceptible to revision."[5] Indeed, since James emphasized the status of faith as a "working hypothesis," he rejected the very notion of dogmatic faith as essentially a contradiction in terms.

With these points in mind, let us turn to consider Darwin's analysis of his scientific observations across the six editions of *The Origin of Species*. Philosophers of science draw an important distinction between a "logic of discovery" and a "logic of confirmation." To simplify what is rather a complex discussion, I might suggest that a "logic of discovery" is about how someone arrives at a scientific hypothesis and a "logic of confirmation" about how that hypothesis is shown to be reliable and realistic.[6] Sometimes hypotheses arise from a long period of reflection on observation; sometimes they come about in a flash of inspiration. Yet if the "logic of discovery" can often be more inspirational than rational, the same is clearly not true of the "logic of justification." Here, any hypothesis—however it is derived—is rigorously and thoroughly checked against what may be observed to determine the degree of empirical fit between theory and observation. There is no reason to suggest that Darwin's notion of natural selection came about in a moment of inspiration: indeed his own account of how he developed the theory makes it clear that it was later reflection on observations that brought about his insight. When he boarded the *Beagle* in 1831, he tells us, he was inclined to the view that the flora and fauna of a given region would be determined by their physical environment. His observations caused him to question this belief and to search for alternative explanations—one of which gradually came to dominate his thinking. Let us listen to Darwin's own account of things.

> During the voyage of the Beagle I had been deeply impressed by discovering in the Pampean formation great fossil animals covered with armour like that on the existing Armadillos; secondly, by the manner in which closely allied animals replace one another in proceeding southwards over the Continent; and thirdly, by the South American character of most of the productions of the Galápagos archipelago, and more especially by the manner in which they differ slightly on each island of the group; none of these islands appearing to be very ancient in the geological sense. It was evident that facts such as these, as well as many others, could be explained on the supposition that species gradually become modified; and the subject haunted me.[7]

As Darwin reflected on his own observations and supplemented them with those of others, the problems and shortcomings of existing explanations became clear. One example was the idea of "special creation," which related to a literal interpretation of the Genesis creation story, offered by religious apologists such as William Paley.[8] Paley's view was essentially that God, in his wisdom, created the world in a manner that displays that wisdom in both design and execution—a notion Paley conveyed using the word *contrivance*. The famous image of God as the divine watchmaker expressed both these ideas of design and skillful fabrication. Though much influenced by Paley, Darwin did not feel his explanation was the best one.

Now the word *best* is difficult to define. Do we mean the

simplest theory? The most elegant? The most natural? The great
English natural philosopher William Whewell (1794-1866) used
a rich visual image to communicate the capacity of a good theory
to make sense of and weave together observations. "The facts are
known but they are insulated and unconnected. . . . The pearls
are there but they will not hang together until some one provides
the string."[9] The "pearls" are the observations and the "string" is
a grand vision of reality, a worldview, that *connects* and *unifies* the
data. A grand theory, Whewell asserted, allows the "colligation
of facts," establishing a new system of relations with each other,
unifying what might have otherwise been considered to be disconnected and isolated observations.

The "pearls" Darwin had accumulated include four categories of observations:

1. Many creatures possess "rudimentary structures," which
   have no apparent or predictable function—such as the nip-
   ples of male mammals, the rudiments of a pelvis and hind
   limbs in snakes and wings on many flightless birds. How
   might these be explained on the basis of Paley's theory,
   which stressed the importance of the individual design of
   species? Why should God design redundancies? Darwin's
   theory accounted for these with ease and elegance.

2. Some species were known to have died out altogether. The
   phenomenon of extinction had been recognized before Darwin and was often explained on the basis of catastrophe
   theories, such as a universal flood, as suggested by the biblical account of Noah. Darwin's theory offered a neater account of the phenomenon.

3. Darwin's research voyage on the *Beagle* had persuaded him
   of the uneven geographical distribution of life forms

throughout the world. In particular, Darwin was impressed by the peculiarities of island populations, such as the finches of the Galápagos islands. Once more, the doctrine of special creation could account for this, yet in a manner that seemed forced and unpersuasive. Darwin's theory offered a much more plausible account of the emergence of these specific populations. *However, the evidence was minimal and is presently entirely refuted by greater evidence.*

4. Various forms of certain living creatures seemed to be adapted to their specific needs. Darwin held that these could best be explained by their emergence and selection in response to evolutionary pressures. Paley's theory of special creation proposed that these creatures were individually designed by God with those specific needs in mind. *which Darwin origins to have anticipated, but did not — bemoaned by pride in his own theory.*

So what could be inferred from these observations? What was the best string on which to thread them?

Darwin was quite clear that his theory of natural selection was not the only possible explanation of the biological data. He did, however, believe that it possessed greater explanatory power than its rivals, such as Paley's doctrine of independent acts of special creation. "Light has been thrown on several facts, which on the belief of independent acts of creation are utterly obscure."[10] *Not any longer!*

Let us pause at this point and consider an aspect of Darwin's scientific method that is often glossed over. Darwin was confronted with a series of observations about the natural world. Indeed, he had even contributed to these himself, through his voyage on the *Beagle*. Yet Darwin's voyage on the *Beagle* was more productive in terms of the ideas it ultimately generated in Darwin's mind than the biological specimens he brought home with him, even though these two are interconnected. The challenge was to find a theoretical framework which could accommodate these observations as simply, elegantly and persuasively as possible. Darwin's method is a textbook case of the method of "inference to the best explanation," which is now widely regarded as lying at the core of the scientific method.[11]

Yet most popular accounts of the scientific method emphasize the importance of prediction. If a theory does not predict, it is not scientific. I think it is important to challenge this approach. Darwin was quite clear that his theory did not predict, and could not predict. That was just the nature of things.[12] In a letter praising the perspicuity of F. W. Hutton (1836-1905), Darwin singled out this point for special comment.

> He is one of the very few who see that the change of species cannot be directly proved, and that the doctrine must sink or swim according as it groups and explains phenomena. It is really curious how few judge it in this way, which is clearly the right way.[13]

Let us linger over that phrase "the doctrine must sink or swim according as it groups and explains phenomena." The nature of the scientific phenomena was such that prediction was not possible for Darwin. This point, of course, led some philosophers of science, most notably Karl Popper, to suggest that Darwinism was not really scientific.[14]   Hah!

Yet more recent studies, especially in the philosophy of biology, have raised interesting questions about whether prediction really is essential to the scientific method. This issue emerged as important in the nineteenth-century debate between William Whewell and John Stuart Mill over the role of induction as a scientific method.[15] Whewell emphasized the importance of predictive novelty as a core element of the scientific method; Mill argued that the difference between prediction of novel observations and theoretical accommodation of existing obser-

vations was purely psychological and had no ultimate episte-
mological significance. The debate, of course, continues. In
their recent discussion of the issue, leading philosophers of biology Christopher Hitchcock and Elliott Sober argue that
while prediction can occasionally be superior to accommodation, this is not always the case.[16] Situations can easily be envi-
sioned where accommodation is superior to prediction. Prediction is neither intrinsically nor invariably to be preferred to
accommodation. The relevance of this point to the scientific
character of Darwin's approach will be obvious. Yet it also
raises some significant doubts about the reliability of popular
accounts of the scientific method.

So how does this bear on William James's idea of faith as a
working hypothesis? I think it is clear that James's emphasis on
the importance of such working hypotheses finds ample exem-
plification in *The Origin of Species*. Darwin's theory had many
weaknesses and loose ends. Nevertheless, he was convinced
that these were difficulties which could be tolerated on account
of the clear explanatory superiority of his approach. His working hypothesis, he believed, was sufficiently robust to resist the
many difficulties that it faced. So what difficulties are we talking about?

Darwin's *Origin of Species* went through six editions, and
Darwin worked constantly to improve his text, adding new
material, amending existing material and, above all, respond-
ing to criticisms in what can only be described as a remarkably
open manner. Those who concern themselves with such details
have shown that of the four thousand sentences in the first edition, Darwin had rewritten three of four by the time of the final sixth edition of 1872. Interestingly, some 60 percent of
these modifications took place in the last two editions, which

introduced some "improvements" that now seem unwise—for example, his incorporation of Herbert Spencer's potentially misleading phrase "the survival of the fittest."[17]

The contents of these successive editions of *The Origin of Species* make it clear that Darwin's new theory faced considerable opposition on many fronts. There is no doubt—for the historical evidence is clear—that some traditional Christian thinkers saw it as a threat to the way they had interpreted their faith. Yet there can also be no doubt—for the historical evidence is equally clear—that other Christians saw Darwin's theory as offering new ways of understanding and parsing traditional Christian ideas. More importantly, however, Darwin's theory provoked scientific controversy, with many scientists of his day raising concerns about the scientific foundations of "natural selection." If the successive editions of the *Origin* are anything to go by, Darwin's theory was frequently assaulted. Yet as historians of science have pointed out, this is the norm, not the exception, in scientific advance. Criticism of a theory is the means by which—to use a Darwinian way of speaking— we discover whether it has survival potential. The reception of a scientific theory is a communal affair in which a "tipping point" is gradually reached through a process of debate and reflection, often linked with additional research programs. Darwin's theory appears to have met more sustained opposition from the scientific community than from its religious counterpart, especially on account of its failure to offer a convincing account of how innovations were transmitted to future generations.

A good example of such scientific criticism is found in Fleeming Jenkin's concerns about "blending inheritance."[18] Jenkin was a Scottish engineer, heavily involved in the business

of developing underwater telephone cables, who identified
what Darwin clearly believed to be a potentially fatal inquiry
flaw in his theory. Jenkin pointed out that on the basis of existing understandings of hereditary transmission, any novelties
would be diluted in subsequent generations. Yet Darwin's theory depended on the transmission, not dilution, of such characteristics. In other words, it lacked a viable understanding of
genetics. Darwin responded to Jenkin in the fifth edition of
the *Origin*. The reply is generally thought to be very weak and
unsatisfactory. But how could it be otherwise? How, indeed.

The answer, of course, lay in the writings of the Austrian
monk and scientist Gregor Mendel, known as the "father of
modern genetics." Yet while Mendel knew about Darwin, Darwin did not know about Mendel. Mendel possessed a copy of
the German translation of the third edition of Darwin's *Origin
of Species*, and marked the following passage with double lines
in the margin. It was clearly of considerable importance to him.
In Darwin's original English, this reads:

> The slight degree of variability in hybrids from the first cross
> or in the first generation, in contrast with their extreme vari-
> ability in the succeeding generations, is a curious fact and de-
> serves attention.[19]

This curiosity would not remain mysterious for much longer,
and Mendel might well have taken some pleasure from the
thought that his theory was able to explain this "curious" fact.[20]
Yet the confluence of Mendel's theory of genetics and Darwin's
theory of natural selection still lay some years in the future.

Even though Darwin did not believe that he had adequately
dealt with all the problems that required resolution, he was
confident that his explanation was the best available. A comment added to the sixth edition makes this point clear. "Inference to
the best."

It can hardly be supposed that a false theory would explain, in so satisfactory a manner as does the theory of natural selection, the several large classes of facts above specified. It has recently been objected that this is an unsafe method of arguing; but it is a method used in judging the common events of life, and has often been used by the greatest natural philosophers.[21]

While recognizing that it lacked rigorous proof, Darwin clearly believed that his theory could be defended on the basis of criteria of acceptance and justification that were already widely used in the natural sciences, and that its explanatory capacity was itself a reliable guide to its truth. As Darwin noted, there were indeed those who argued that his was an "unsafe method of arguing"—but, in an important anticipation of some of William James's points, Darwin correctly points out that it is widely used in everyday situations. We often find ourselves trusting a way of thinking, believing it to be true, but not being able to offer the decisive proof that some—such as W. G. Clifford in Darwin's day and Richard Dawkins in our own day—seem to think is essential for an opinion to be held with integrity.

Darwin was aware that his scientific explanation lacked the logical rigor of mathematical proofs and that any theoretical account of what was observed would always be provisional. That is no criticism of Darwin, and it is no criticism of science. It's just the way things are. I have scientific colleagues who believe passionately in the multiverse, and others who believe with equal passion, integrity and intellectual excellence in a single universe. The evidence is not unequivocal, and both positions can be maintained. But both, I would suggest, cannot be right. What some scientists today believe to be true will one day be shown to be wrong. But that's how science develops.

And William James's idea of faith as a "working hypothesis" fits both the theory and practice of science surprisingly well.

As historians and philosophers of science keep telling us, the positivist notion of science proving its theories stands at some considerable distance from the reality of scientific practice, and it certainly does not apply to Darwin's scientific method. The great theories of classical physics, widely regarded as settled and stable toward the end of Darwin's life, underwent complete revision in the twentieth century through the rise of quantum mechanics and the theory of relativity. But we don't stop doing science because our successors may show our present theories to be wrong, and we can at least take consolation in knowing that future theories tend to incorporate, rather than reject, what is best in older theories.

So what of Darwin's religious faith? Did his theory of evolution turn him into an atheist crusader against religious belief, as some seem to suggest? Sadly, Darwin's authority and example are continually invoked to justify metaphysical and theological claims that go far beyond anything that he himself expressed in, or associated with, his evolutionary biology. Happily, the fundamentally *historical* question of Darwin's religious views is relatively easy to answer, thanks to the intensive scholarly study of Darwin and his Victorian context in the last few decades.[22] The excellent online Darwin Project has a section which brings together the most important historical evidence in a way that seems to me to be historically objective and trustworthy.[23] Let me try to summarize this vast body of literature as simply as I can.

First, it seems clear to me that Darwin's religious faith altered as he becomes older. I certainly see a change in its content; I think I am also right in seeing a decline in its fervency.

But - How many became atheist because of the fabulist not Darwin was writing?

Let us consider the contents of that faith, looking first at Darwin's early religious views.

We cannot really hope to understand the young Darwin without seeing his ideas through a refracting lens, shaped by the writings of William Paley and others influenced by him, such as John Bird Sumner (1780-1862), who was later to become Archbishop of Canterbury. There is a physical and intellectual continuity between the young Darwin and Paley: not only did Darwin occupy the same room as Paley had before him at Christ College, Cambridge; Darwin refers with warmth to Paley's classic *Natural Theology*, which, as we've seen, in many ways defines the position that he eventually believes he must reject. Paley's detailed descriptions of the adaptations to be found in plants and animals—such as the human eye—seem to have become normative for Darwin. Darwin may have exaggerated slightly in stating that he had committed Paley to memory; nevertheless, echoes of Paley's works are found throughout *The Origin of Species*. Stephen Jay Gould has pointed out how Darwin's statement of his principle of natural selection is deeply indebted to the language and imagery found in Paley's writings, even though Darwin would later draw some very different conclusions.[24]

Indeed, Darwin himself adopted Paley's heavily loaded term *contrivance* in one of his own works, dealing with the methods of fertilization of orchids. Darwin's *On the Various Contrivances by Which British and Foreign Orchids Are Fertilised by Insects* appeared in 1862, shortly after the appearance of *The Origin of Species*. Although it was not a commercial success, it had the potential to make a significant contribution to the debate about the implications of Darwin's theory for natural theology. The distinguished American botanist Asa Gray (1810-1888) is reported as declaring that "if the Orchid-book (with a few tri-fling omissions) had appeared before the 'Origin', the author would have been canonised rather than anathematised by the natural theologians." Indeed, a review in the *Literary Church-man* had only one criticism to make of this work—namely, that Darwin's expression of admiration at the "contrivances" found in orchids amounted to an unnecessarily indirect manner of saying, "O Lord, how manifold are Thy works."[25]

It should not surprise us that many natural theologians took the view that Darwin rescued Paley's theory by placing it on a firmer intellectual foundation through rectifying a faulty and ultimately fatal premise. Charles Kingsley, then a canon of Westminster Abbey, was certainly one to take this viewpoint. In his 1871 lecture "On the Natural Theology of the Future," Kingsley singled out Darwin's work on orchids as "a most valu-able addition to natural theology."[26] Insisting that the word *creation* implies process as much as event, Kingsley went on to argue that Darwin's theory clarified the mechanism of cre-ation. "We knew of old that God was so wise that he could make all things; but, behold, he is so much wiser than even that, that he can make all things make themselves."[27] Where Paley thought of a static creation, Kingsley argued that Darwin made it possible to see creation as a dynamic process directed by divine providence. Yet as subsequent developments made clear, Darwin did not himself share Kingsley's confidence con-cerning Paley's natural theology. However, it is important to appreciate that Darwin's intellectual anxiety about Paley's ap-proach antedates his reflections on natural selection and is re-ligious rather than scientific in character. Let me explain.

Paley's approach to nature is optimistic and positive. Nature exudes evidence of divine wisdom. So what then of evil? Or

So what then of Satan?

suffering? Kingsley certainly held that these could be incorporated within Paley's approach to natural theology.[28] Yet Darwin's travels on the *Beagle* led him to witness events that called into question his early belief in divine providence. For example, while in South America, Darwin witnessed at first hand the terrible struggle for existence faced by the natives of the Tierra del Fuego; he saw the devastating effects of an earthquake; and he began to grasp the magnitude of the staggering numbers of species that had become extinct—each of which, according to Paley, was providentially created and valued by God. We can see here the beginnings of the erosion of any belief in divine providence, which would become characteristic of the later Darwin. If a crisis point was reached, it may have been through the death of Darwin's daughter Annie in 1851, at the age of ten, which Darwin's biographer James Moore sees as marking a watershed in Darwin's religious convictions.[29] Yet the origins of this development date from much earlier in his life.

This brings us to our second point. Darwin's religious beliefs unquestionably veered away from what we might loosely call "Christian orthodoxy." Yet we do not find anything remotely resembling the aggressive and ridiculing form of atheism we unfortunately encounter in some of those who have presented themselves as his champions in more recent times. Many have praised the prescience and cool neutrality of *The Origin of Species*, noting its Olympian social and political detachment and scrupulous religious neutrality. It is in Darwin's letters that we must turn for illumination of both the fluctuations of his religious beliefs over time and his reluctance to comment on religious matters, including his own personal beliefs. Yet when the context demanded it, Darwin seems to have been willing not merely to go on record concerning but to emphasize the consilience of religious faith and the theory of natural selection. *That quite a "consilience"!*

It would be tedious to illustrate this in detail. A representative example lies to hand in his reference to "laws impressed on matter by the Creator," which is given a higher profile in the second edition of the *Origin* than in the first.[30] This certainly points to a deistic God rather than a trinitarian God. But there is not even the whiff of a personal atheism here. While some might argue that Darwin may have made it possible to be an intellectually fulfilled atheist, Darwin did not himself draw that conclusion. I find it very difficult to believe that his references to a Creator in *The Origin of Species* were simply contrived to mollify his audience, representing crude deceptions aimed at masking a private atheism that Darwin feared might discredit his theory in the eyes of the religious public. My own reading of the evidence is that Darwin regarded religious beliefs as a private matter and was reluctant to talk about his own religious commitments. Yet the needs of the situation regularly obliged him to say something on this matter. The evidence, I believe, points to reluctant, painful and diplomatic self-disclosure of Darwin's beliefs, not the fabrication or manipulation of those beliefs for tactical purposes.

Belief in God "is a private matter." That's news to those who faithfully fulfill Christ's "Great Commission."

The core theme of this chapter has been Darwin's belief that his theory of natural selection offered the best explanation of what could be observed in the living natural world. It is not true to state that science believes only what has been empirically proven. At points, inference is necessary, in which an hypothesis (such as a "missing link" or an unobserved entity such as "natural selection") is postulated as the "best explanation" of known facts or established observations. This is an accepted norm of scientific reasoning and is not controversial. *But, shouldn't be controversial? "Natural Selection" is a pretty dogmatic concept. And if you hold it firmly tends to cut off any opposition! Just ask Richard Dawkins.*

Yet it is important to note that the same process can be also seen at work in religious thinking, which also aims to give the best explanation of what it observes. To quote William James again, religious faith is basically "faith in the existence of an unseen order of some kind in which the riddles of the natural order may be found and explained."[31] Although some persist in portraying religious belief as irrational, the fact is that its proponents regard it as eminently reasonable. In any classical philosophical theism or natural theology, God would be proposed as the best explanation of the way things are.

Both the natural sciences and religions offer what they believe to be warranted, coherent and reliable explanations of the world. Darwin, as we have seen, believed firmly that the explanatory power of his theory was such that it could coexist with anomalies and potential threats. This is a reminder that both scientific and religious theories find themselves confronted with mysteries, puzzles and anomalies which may give rise to intellectual or existential tensions, but do not require their abandonment. In the case of Christianity, I would judge that the greatest such anomaly is the existence of pain and suffering.[32] Yet I believe that the theory is big enough ultimately to be able to embrace and accommodate this anomaly, even though at present the manner of its resolution seems less than clear. Neither Darwin's theory nor Christian theology can really be said to predict; *pre-* they do, however, accommodate what is known about the world, *diot/* even though both experience points of tension. *redact*

To bring out the theological importance of this parallel, let us consider two scenarios. As we have seen, Darwin held that the ideas set out in *The Origin of Species* offer an excellent and deeply compelling account of the diversity of life forms on the earth. Yet there are many difficulties in its path. How could

* The existence of pain is an anomaly only to the scientist or theologian who refuses, overlooks, or denies the existence of Satan. Or who is embarrassed to acknowledge the "Explanatory Power"!

change be transmitted from one generation to another? Darwin offered an explanation of how different species come into existence. Though speciation—the formation of a new species by the accumulation of mutations—had never been demonstrated in real life or under laboratory conditions, Darwin held on to the theory, believing that its explanatory ability and coherence are sufficient to justify it, and that the difficulty would one day be resolved. *Ah, yes . . .*

Consider now the case of a Christian, who holds that a theistic worldview, especially one which takes full account of the doctrine of the incarnation, offers a compelling and attractive understanding of things. The issue of pain and suffering in the world remains something of a puzzle, and at times troubles her considerably. Yet she holds on to her faith, believing that its explanatory ability and coherence are sufficient to justify it, and that the difficulty will one day be resolved.[33] In each case, there is a common structure of an explanation with anomalies, which are not regarded as endangering the theory by its proponents but are seen as puzzles that will be resolved at a later stage. Neither theory predicts; both accommodate what can be observed. In celebrating Darwin, we also affirm the possibility of believing in a theory, a way of making sense of things, a "working hypothesis," which is not finally confirmed and may not ultimately be capable of final confirmation—yet which is found to be reliable. *Reliable?! please!*

The point here is that a theory of sufficient explanatory power has earned the right to coexist with observations that do not accord with it and may at times even seem to be in conflict with it. In the end, some theories die because of their incapacity to deal with such anomalies. Darwin knew this; he also believed that his theory would be shown to be able to

✱ Isn't it already "resolved." Instead, hasn't always been resolved? Why did Christ come to earth? Why was He rejected and crucified? And why on earth was He then RESURRECTED? Evidence that demands a

cope with them, even if the final vindication of his theory lay in the future. Dare I suggest that the same is true for Christianity, which currently affirms that we see things through a glass darkly (1 Corinthians 13:12), but rejoices that we shall one day see them with the clarity that is found only within the New Jerusalem?

Let me draw this chapter to a close by citing some words from the first edition of the *Origin*, which are retained throughout subsequent editions. As he pauses to allow his readers to catch up with him, Darwin lays the groundwork for his argument that his new theory can coexist with anomalies and apparent contradictions. I believe these words apply with equal force to the Christian vision of reality.✳

> A crowd of difficulties will have occurred to the reader. Some of them are so grave that to this day I can never reflect on them without being staggered; but, to the best of my judgement, the greater number are only apparent, and those that are real are not, I think, fatal to my theory.[34]

✳This is highly sophisticated "Special Pleading." But it is only that and nothing else. The vision of Christianity has nothing whatever to ~~do~~ with "Natural Selection", and can never have. McGrath fails to acknowledge this: He fails to separate the "sheep from the goats." This is quite a telling failure: "And He will set the sheep on His right hand, but the goats on His right." And, etc.   —Mt. 25: 32.

verdict!

9

AUGUSTINE OF HIPPO ON
CREATION AND EVOLUTION

THE DARWIN CELEBRATIONS OF 2009 showcased many religious issues, one being how the great creation narratives of the Old Testament are to be interpreted.[1] Many Christians assume that the church's long tradition of faithful biblical exegesis has always treated the biblical creation accounts as straightforward historical accounts of how everything came into being. In fact, things are rather more interesting, and in this chapter we shall explore why.

I have already spoken several times of one of the most respected early Christian biblical scholars, Augustine of Hippo (354-430). Augustine interpreted Scripture a thousand years before the "Scientific Revolution" of our modern period and fifteen hundred years before Darwin's *Origin of Species*. There is just no way Augustine can be considered to have "accommodated" or "compromised" his biblical interpretation in order to fit in new theories about the big bang or natural selection. He set out to interpret Scripture on its own terms, faithfully and carefully. In fact, he even criticized those who tried to adapt their biblical interpretation to the latest scientific theories. The important thing was to let Scripture speak for itself.

Augustine wrestled with Genesis 1–2 throughout his career. There are at least four points in his writings where he attempts to develop a detailed, systematic account of how these chapters are to be understood. Each is subtly different. Here I would like to consider *The Literal Meaning of Genesis,* which was written between 401 and 415. Augustine intended this to be a "literal" commentary (meaning "in the sense intended by the author").

Augustine discerns the following themes in his reading of Scripture and weaves them together into his account of creation. God brought everything into existence in a single moment of creation. Yet the created order is not static. God endowed it with the capacity to develop. Augustine uses the image of a dormant seed to help his readers grasp this point. God creates seeds, which will grow and develop at the right time. Using more technical language, Augustine asks his readers to think of the created order as containing divinely embedded causalities that emerge or evolve at a later stage. Yet Augustine has no time for any notion of random or arbitrary changes within creation. The development of God's creation is always subject to God's sovereign providence. The God who planted the seeds at the moment of creation also governs and directs the time and place of their growth.

Augustine argues that the first creation account (Genesis 1:1–2:3) cannot be interpreted in isolation but must be set alongside the second creation account (Genesis 2:4-25), as well as every other statement about the creation found in Scripture. For example, Augustine suggests that Psalm 33:6-9 speaks of an instantaneous creation of the world through God's creative Word, while John 5:17 points to a God who is still active within creation. God created the world in an instant but continues to develop and mold it, even to the present day. This leads Augustine to suggest that the six days of creation are not to be understood chronologically. Rather, they are a way of categorizing God's work of creation. They provide a framework for the classification of the elements of the created world so they may be better understood and appreciated.

Augustine was deeply concerned that biblical interpreters might get locked into reading the Bible according to the scientific assumptions of the age. This, of course, is what happened during the Copernican controversies of the late sixteenth century. Biblical interpreters, who already held that the sun revolved around the earth, read the Bible in the light of this controlling assumption. Unsurprisingly, the Bible was then held to support a geocentric view of the solar system. Some church leaders mistakenly interpreted challenges to this erroneous idea in the sixteenth century as a challenge to the authority of the Bible itself. It was not, of course. It was a challenge to one specific interpretation of the Bible—an interpretation, as it happened, in urgent need of review.

Augustine anticipated this point a millennium earlier. Certain biblical passages, he insisted, can legitimately be understood in different ways. The important thing is that these interpretations must not be wedded to prevailing scientific theories. Otherwise, the Bible becomes the prisoner of what was once believed to be scientifically true.

> In matters that are so obscure and far beyond our vision, we find in Holy Scripture passages which can be interpreted in very different ways without prejudice to the faith we have received. In such cases, we should not rush in headlong and so firmly take our stand on one side that, if further progress in the

search for truth justly undermines our position, we too fall with it.

Augustine's approach allowed theology to avoid becoming trapped in a prescientific worldview. It is important to appreciate that he faced significant cultural pressure to adapt his biblical interpretations to prevailing thinking. For example, many leading contemporary scientists of the late classical era regarded the Christian view of creation from nothing *(ex nihilo)* as utter nonsense. Claudius Galen (129-200), celebrity physician to the Roman emperor Marcus Aurelius, dismissed it as a logical and metaphysical absurdity. Augustine noted the resistance of his culture to this notion, but believed that the biblical texts required him to affirm it. It was an integral part of the web of Christian doctrine, a coherent set of interlocking ideas.

This doctrine of "creation from nothing" had some important implications. For example, Augustine argues that Scripture teaches that time is part of the created order. God created space and time together, so time must therefore be thought of as one of God's creatures and servants. Time is an element of the created order; timelessness, on the other hand, is the essential feature of eternity.

So what was God doing before he created the universe? Augustine undermines the question by pointing out that God did not bring creation into being at a certain definite moment in time, because time did not exist prior to creation. For Augustine, eternity is a realm without space or time. Interestingly, this is precisely the state of affairs that many scientists believe existed before the big bang.

So what are the implications of this classic Christian interpretation of Genesis for the Darwin celebrations? One point is particularly obvious. Augustine's exegesis of Genesis shows that a "faithful" or "authentic" interpretation of the biblical texts concerning creation does not necessarily demand a six-day period of creation. The opening chapter of Genesis must, Augustine argues, be set in context—initially, in the context of Genesis 2, and subsequently in the context of Scripture as a whole. For Augustine the big question is this: what way of articulating the doctrine of creation makes sense of *all* the biblical statements on the matter and not simply the first chapter of Genesis? His own answer is hardly the last word on the matter. But it is an excellent starting point for reflection. Above all, it shows the importance of weaving the total witness of Scripture into a coherent doctrine of creation and not limiting this to Scripture's first few dozen verses.

Augustine does not limit God's creative action to the primordial act of origination. God is, he insists, still working within the world, directing its continuing development and unfolding its potential. There are two "moments" in the creation: a primary act of origination and a continuing process of providential guidance. Creation is thus not a completed past event. God is working even now, in the present, Augustine writes, sustaining and directing the unfolding of the "generations that he laid up in creation when it was first established."

This twofold focus on the creation allows us to read Genesis in a way that affirms that God created everything from nothing, in an instant. However, it also helps us affirm that the universe has been created with an intended capacity to develop, under God's sovereign guidance. Thus the primordial state of creation does not correspond to what we presently observe. For Augustine God created a universe that was deliberately designed to develop and evolve. The blueprint for that evolution is not arbitrary but is programmed into the very fabric of creation. God's providence superintends the continuing unfolding of the created order.

Earlier Christian writers noted how the first Genesis creation narrative speaks of the earth and the waters "bringing forth" living creatures. They concluded that this pointed to God's endowing the natural order with a capacity to generate living things. Augustine takes this idea further: God created the world complete with a series of dormant powers, which were actualized at appropriate moments through divine providence. Augustine argues that Genesis 1:12 implies that the earth received the power or capacity to produce things by itself: "Scripture has stated that the earth brought forth the crops and the trees causally, in the sense that it received the power of bringing them forth."

Where some might think of the creation as God's insertion of new kinds of plants and animals ready-made into an already existing world, Augustine rejects this as inconsistent with the overall witness of Scripture. Rather, God must be thought of as creating in that very first moment the potencies for all the kinds of living things to come later, including humanity.

This means that the first creation account describes the instantaneous bringing into existence of primal matter, including causal resources for further development. The second account explores how these causal possibilities emerged and developed from the earth. Taken together, the two Genesis creation accounts declare that God made the world instantaneously, while envisioning that the various kinds of living things would make their appearance gradually over time—as they were intended to by their Creator.

The image of the "seed" implies that the original creation contained within it the potential for all the living kinds to subsequently emerge. This does not mean that God created the world incomplete or imperfect, in that "what God originally established in causes, he subsequently fulfilled in effects." This process of development, Augustine declares, is governed by fundamental laws, which reflect the will of their Creator: "God has established fixed laws governing the production of kinds and qualities of beings, and bringing them out of concealment into full view."

I must emphasize at this point that neither Augustine nor his age believed in the evolution of species. There were no reasons at that time for anyone to believe in this notion. Yet Augustine developed a theological framework that could accommodate this later scientific development, though his theological commitments would prevent him from accepting any idea of the development of the universe as a random or lawless process. For this reason Augustine would have opposed the strict Darwinian notion of random variations, insisting that God's providence is deeply involved throughout, directing a process in manners and ways that lie beyond full human comprehension.

Let's be clear about this: Augustine isn't playing at being a scientist. Nor is he confusing science and theology. Augustine is not contradicting a scientific account of origins; rather, he is setting it within a theological scaffolding. Scientific analysis clarifies how cosmic development takes place; Augustine's theological framework clarifies how God is involved in this development.

Augustine's approach to creation is neither liberal nor accommodationist, but is deeply biblical, both in its substance and intentions. It needs to be taken into account when Christians reflect on the themes of creation and evolution. Sloganeering and grandstanding will not help us at all here. Examining the long Christian tradition of biblical exegesis will.

DOES RELIGION
POISON EVERYTHING?

The New Atheism and Religious Belief

I‍s RELIGION INTRINSICALLY EVIL?[1] This view, energetically affirmed with an almost religious enthusiasm in Richard Dawkins's book *The God Delusion* (2006) has achieved widespread circulation in recent years.[2] It is vigorously reasserted in Christopher Hitchens's *God Is Not Great: How Religion Poisons Everything* (2007).[3] "Religion poisons everything" is a rhetorically charged message that appeals to a certain type of middle-class liberal rationalist. The faults of the world are to be laid at the door of backward-looking superstitions, which hold the world back from its rational and scientific destiny. Eliminate religion and the world will be a better place. Religion has led only to violence, intellectual dishonesty, oppression and social division.

These attitudes are, of course, shaped by a controlling metanarrative that is characteristic of the new atheism. At the philosophical level this holds that metaphysical austerity is a reliable indicator of truth and that all "unevidenced beliefs" represent a deluded "blind faith." At the sociological level it is held that religion is socially divisive and leads to oppression and violence. At the personal level it holds that those who entertain religious belief are deluded and potentially dangerous to society at large. This simplistic metanarrative can only be sustained by doing violence to the facts of history, the norms of evidence-based argument and the realities of contemporary experience. Hitchens achieves this feat largely by ignoring any evidence to the contrary and papering over the many cracks in his argument with aggressive bullying rhetoric that intimidates those who wish to challenge him on rational or historical grounds.

Yet it is the sociological aspect of the new atheist critique of religion that appears to have gained most cultural traction. On this view, religion is intrinsically and necessarily dangerous, poisonous and evil. This somewhat crude sound bite is ideally attuned to a media-driven culture which prefers breezy slogans to serious analysis. It resonates deeply, perhaps at a subrational level, with the fears of many in Western culture. The suicide attacks by Islamic fanatics on the World Trade Center in New York and elsewhere, now universally referred to as "9/11," are seen as a surefire demonstration of the intrinsic evil of religion. Lurking within every religious believer lies a potential terrorist. Get rid of religion and the world will be a safer place.

Generalizations like this are found throughout Richard Dawkins's *God Delusion*, Christopher Hitchens's *God Is not Great*, and Sam Harris's *End of Reason*.[4] Harris offers his own readings of central religious texts—such as the Bible and the Qur'an—to demonstrate that they possess an innate propensity to generate violence. Yet there is no attempt to analyze how these texts are interpreted and applied within their respective religious communities.

For example, Dawkins tells us that to take the Bible seriously is to "strictly observe the sabbath and think it just and proper to execute anyone who chose not to." Or to "execute disobedient children."[5] It is a simple fact that Christians do not interpret, and have not interpreted, these Old Testament injunctions as binding for the church. Dawkins appears to assume that his religiously alienated readers know so little about Christianity that they would believe that Christians are in the habit of stoning people to death if they work on a Sunday. A reality check is clearly in order.

Furthermore, the new atheism simply assumes, without any serious argumentation or appeal to evidence, that the naturalistic worldview proposed as a replacement for religion will generate more happiness, compassion or peace than religion can. Sam Harris's *End of Reason* bristles with the curious and highly problematic idea that scientists have a keener or deeper appreciation than religious people of how to deal with personal or moral problems. Yet such is the force of his rhetoric that such evidential deficits are airbrushed out of the picture.

So what is "new" about the new atheism? An innocent reader might assume that this movement had discovered new scientific evidence or fresh philosophical arguments that demonstrated that God was the arbitrary and meaningless construction of the human mind. Yet it soon becomes clear that there are no new lines of reasoning here. The old, familiar and somewhat tired arguments of the past are recycled and rehashed. What is new is the aggressiveness of the rhetoric, which often seems to degenerate into bullying and hectoring. It serves a convenient purpose, by papering over the obvious evidential gaps and argumentative lapses that are so characteristic of this movement. But it does little to encourage anyone to take atheism with intellectual seriousness. The philosophical roots of Dawkins's atheism, for example, are easily exposed as shallow, uninformed and severely vulnerable.[6]

Let us look more closely at this core claim that religion is evil. Such is its cultural power that it tends to be assumed, rather than demonstrated, by those who advocate it. This I think tells us rather more about contemporary cultural prejudices and biases than about religion itself. In fact, it turns out to be an article of faith, a belief which can only be sustained by highly selective use of evidence and what comes close to manipulation of history for the purposes of advancing an aggressively atheist agenda.

As explained earlier, when I was an atheist myself, things seemed admirably clear. Growing up in Northern Ireland, infamous in the late 1960s for its religious tensions and violence, it appeared obvious to me that if there were no religion, there would be no religious violence. I bought into the now outdated Enlightenment view, which we have seen charmingly yet not a little uncritically echoed in the manifestoes of new atheism, that humanity was innocent and disinclined to violence until religion came along. Get rid of religion and humanity could rediscover a golden age of reason and toleration. This theme is particularly evident in Hitchens's *God Is Not Great*.

It's a neat idea that makes for great rhetoric. Yet it is indefensible in the face of the evidence, rather like believing in Santa Claus or the tooth fairy. A core belief of the new atheism, which it persistently tries to represent as scientific fact, is that religion is the cause of the ills of humanity. But what is the evidence for this assertion?

"RELIGION," A FALSE UNIVERSAL

The first point to make is simple: "religion" is a false universal. Individual religions exist; "religion" doesn't. The Enlightenment was characterized by a love of universals, most famously stated in the idea of a universal human reason, whose fundamental characteristics were independent of history and culture. For the Enlightenment this universal human reason could be the basis of a true, global ethic and philosophy, which would sweep aside irrational superstitions as relics of a barbarous past. In the end this noble idea proved to be unworkable in that human patterns of reasoning turned out to be much more culturally conditioned than had been realized.

The key point here is that the Enlightenment understandably yet wrongly regarded "religion" as a universal category. During the period of colonial expansion, many Europeans came across worldviews that differed from their own and chose to label them as "religions." In fact, many of these were better regarded as philosophies of life, such as Confucianism. Some were explicitly nontheistic. Yet the Enlightenment belief in a universal notion called "religion" led to these being forced into the same mold. It is increasingly agreed that definitions of religion tend to reflect the agendas and bias of those who propose them. There is still no definition of *religion* that commands scholarly assent.[7] Indeed, the noted English philosopher Mary Midgely argued that evolution, as developed by Richard Dawkins and others, had itself become a religious belief system.[8]

Religion clearly belongs to what the philosopher Donald Brown calls "universals of classification," rather than to "universals of content."[9] "Universals of content" have shared core beliefs; "universals of classification," on the other hand, share common patterns, but not necessarily individual beliefs. They have fuzzy boundaries and lack easily distinguishable core convictions.

For these reasons there has recently been concerted criticism of this unhelpful and deeply problematic approach, which underlies "pluralist" approaches to religion as much as atheism.[10] In its more naive forms, pluralism holds that all religions represent equally valid responses to the same divine reality; in its more naive forms, the new atheism holds that they all represent equally invalid and delusional responses to a fictional nonreality. In reality the porous and imprecise concept of "religion" extends far beyond those who believe in God, embracing a wide range of beliefs and values.

RELIGIONS AND WORLDVIEWS

It is also vitally important to make a distinction between a *religion* and a *worldview*. This is a distinction that the new atheism singularly fails to make or defend. Both religions (such as Christianity) and secular worldviews (such as Marxism) demand allegiance from their followers. The most successful worldviews incorporate religious elements, even if they are fundamentally secular in their outlook—as in the Soviet Union's use of quasi-religious rituals to mark essentially secular events.

The historian Martin Marty, noting the lack of any viable definition of religion, identifies five features that he holds to be characteristic of religion; all five, he notes, are also characteristic of political movements.[11] It is not unreasonable to point out that if religion is dangerous on this count, then so is politics. There can be (and are) political fanatics, just as there can be (and are) religious fanatics. The problem is fanaticism, not religion or politics themselves. The dark and aggressive tone of the new atheism critique of religion suggests that fanaticism may not be limited to the ranks of those who defend religion.

The new atheism, of course, argues that religious world-views offer motivations for violence that are not paralleled elsewhere—for example, the thought of entering paradise after a suicidal attack. Yet this conclusion is premature and needs very careful nuancing. For Harris and Hitchens it is obvious that religious belief leads directly to suicide bombings. It's a view that Hitchens's less critical secular readers will applaud, provided they haven't read the empirical studies of why people are driven to suicide bombings in the first place.[12] Even Daw-kins is cautious at this point, suggesting that religion may only be one of the factors involved.

As Robert Pape showed in his definitive account of the mo-tivations of such attacks, based on surveys of every known case of suicide bombing since 1980, religious belief of any kind does not appear to be either a necessary or a sufficient condition to create suicide bombers.[13] The infamous "suicide vest," for ex-ample, was invented by Tamil Tigers back in 1991, leading to a large number of suicide attacks from this ethnic group. Pape's analysis of the evidence suggests that the fundamental motiva-tion for suicide bombings appears to be political, not religious—namely, the desire to force the withdrawal of foreign forces oc-cupying land believed to belong to an oppressed people who have seriously limited military resources at their disposal.

The new atheism offers a superficial explanation for sui-cide bombings, designed to resonate with cultural anxieties about the heightened profile of religion in the United States and many parts of the world. Yet it is not a sustainable analy-sis and does little to help us understand why these bombings arise and what can be done to prevent them. They have sim-ply been hijacked as part of a crude atheist apologetic, rather than taken seriously as a cultural and social phenomenon. Happily, there are many serious studies, particularly from an anthropological perspective (including the important work of Scott Atran of the University of Michigan), which point in more realistic and informed directions.[14] For Atran the way to stop suicide bombings is not the excoriation of religion, still less its suppression, but the empowerment of religious moderates.

As Richard Wentz points out, the real issue here is absolutism.[15] People create and sustain absolutes out of fear of their own limitations, and people react with violence when others do not accept them. Religion may have a tendency toward absolutism, but the same tendency is innate in any human attempt to find or create meaning, especially when it is challenged. The key thing here, it seems, is not the ideas or values, but the dedication, even fanaticism, of those who follow them.

ATHEISM AND MODERNITY

As we shall note in the final chapter of this book, the new atheism is a superb example of a modern metanarrative—a totalizing view of things, locked into the worldview of the Enlightenment. The new atheism wants to take us back to what it portrays as the cool rationalism and sanity of the Enlightenment. Yet it fails to confront even a representative sample of the many contemporary critics of Enlightenment rationalism. It is much easier to defend a position when its critics are ignored. The new atheism is widely dismissed on account of its deeply flawed and biased account of religion; it seems we must extend that criticism by pointing out its total failure to confront the deep flaws, all of which have been known for some time, in its positive proposals.

Philosophical and cultural critics of the Enlightenment have exposed its intellectual indefensibility on the one hand, and its intolerance toward alternative worldviews, which it declares to be irrational on the other. Modernity, its critics argue, created an intellectual context that legitimates suppression of what it regards as aberrant or irrational beliefs. The new atheism is thoroughly modernist, excoriating postmodernism precisely because it challenges and subverts its core assumptions.

The new atheism advocates a "return to the Enlightenment" without any attempt to confront the dark side of modernity. Where in the manifestoes of the movement is there any attempt to deal with the influential view, set out by Theodor Adorno and Max Horkheimer, that the sources of twentieth-century totalitarianism lie in the European Enlightenment—specifically, in its allegedly instrumental and totalizing conception of reason?[16] The same Enlightenment that the new atheism asks us to accept as a model of toleration and excellence is now charged with having fostered oppression and violence, and having colluded with totalitarianism, by its postmodern critics. The new atheism deals with this by ignoring it. Hitchens, for example, woodenly and somewhat implausibly persists in locating the roots of totalitarianism in religion. There is no recognition of the deeper truth that a significant incentive to oppression and even violence lies to hand in precisely the worldview that he advocates as the solution to our ills.[17]

RELIGION AND VIOLENCE

If there is a serious point to be made by the new atheism, it is that religion—or, if we avoid exaggeration, certain forms of religion—possess a capacity to transcendentalize normal human conflicts and disagreements, transforming them into cosmic battles of good and evil, in which the authority and will of a transcendent reality is implicated. If God tells you to kill someone, who can argue with that? Although this point is often made in a muddled and overstated manner, there is a serious point that needs to be considered: why might someone think that God would order them to kill someone?

Now, as a Christian I regard the idea that all religions teach pretty much the same thing as fatuous, but it is curiously favored both by political and theological liberals (anxious to elevate the generic concept of religion above any specific religious system to facilitate an inclusionist agenda) and atheists (who are anxious to show that religion is generically and intrinsically evil by singling out a single religion as representative of all, as in Sam Harris's stereotypical account of Islam).

As a Christian I hold that the face, will and character of God are fully disclosed in Jesus of Nazareth.[18] And Jesus of Nazareth did no violence to anyone. He was the object, not the agent, of violence. Instead of meeting violence with violence, rage with rage, Christians are asked to "turn the other cheek" and "not to let the sun go down on their anger." This speaks of more than the mere elimination of the roots of violence; it relates to its *transfiguration*. Does the God and Father of our Lord Jesus Christ command anyone to kill in his name? Certainly some Christians argued so, especially during the age of the Crusades. But that belief is deeply problematic when confronted with the person of Christ. Christ commanded the sword to be put down, not to be taken up, in His defense. The contrast with Islam is particularly telling at this point.

The importance of the witness of Christ on this matter can be seen in a tragic event in North America that took place in October 2006, within a week of the publication of Dawkins's *God Delusion*. A gunman broke into an Amish school in Pennsylvania and gunned down a group of schoolgirls. Five of the young girls died. The Amish are a Protestant religious group who repudiate any form of violence on account of their understanding of the absolute moral authority of the person and teaching of Jesus of Nazareth. When those unfortunate schoolchildren were murdered, the Amish community urged forgiveness. There would be no violence, no revenge—only the offering of forgiveness. The gunman's widow spoke, gratefully and movingly, of how this provided the "healing" that she and her three children "so desperately needed."

Richard Dawkins is nauseatingly condescending about the Amish in his *God Delusion*. Yet I cannot help but feel that he misses something rather important in his blanket dismissal of their significance. If the world was more like Jesus of Nazareth, violence might indeed be a thing of the past. But that does not appear to be an answer that Dawkins feels comfortable with.

ATHEIST VIOLENCE AGAINST RELIGION

At this point we need to explore another theme that is conveniently glossed over by the new atheist manifestoes. *What about atheist violence against religion?* As someone who grew up in Northern Ireland, I know about religious violence only too well. There is no doubt that religion can generate violence. But it's not alone in this. The history of the twentieth century has given us a frightening awareness of how political extremism can equally cause violence. In Latin America, millions of people seem to have "disappeared" as a result of ruthless campaigns of violence by right-wing politicians and their militias. In Cambodia, Pol Pot eliminated millions in the name of socialism. Worldviews, whether religious or secular, have the power to inspire people to the use of force, violence and repression.[19]

The rise of the Soviet Union was of particular significance. Lenin regarded the intellectual, cultural and physical elimination of religion as central to the socialist revolution and put in place measures designed to eradicate religious beliefs through the "protracted use of violence." One of the greatest tragedies of this dark era in human history is that those who sought to eliminate religious belief through violence and oppression believed they were justified in doing so.[20] They were accountable to no higher authority than the state.

This problem was anticipated by Fyodor Dostoyevsky in his great novel *The Devils*. The most important character in the novel is Kirillov, who argues that the nonexistence of God legitimates all forms of actions. The importance of this theme for Dostoyevsky is best appreciated from his 1878 letter to Nikolai Ozmidov, in which he sets out the implications of atheism for morality:

> Now assume that there is no God, or immortality of the soul.
> Now tell me, why should I live righteously and do good deeds,
> if I am to die entirely on earth? . . . And if that is so, why
> shouldn't I (as long as I can rely on my cleverness and agility to
> avoid being caught by the law) cut another man's throat, rob
> and steal?[21]

In *The Devils*, Dostoyevsky places a similar line of argument in the mouth of the somewhat eccentric character Alexei Nilych Kirillov: if there is no God, it follows that he, Kirillov, is God. This puzzles Pyotr Stephanovich, who asks him to explain what he means. Kirillov responds as follows:

> If God exists, then everything is His will, and I can do nothing
> of my own apart from His will. If there's no God, then every-
> thing is my will, and I'm bound to express my self-will.[22]

Since the idea of God is a pure human invention, Kirillov reasons that he is free to do as he pleases. There is no higher authority to whom he is ultimately accountable or who is able to negate his totalitarian moral self-assertion.

The first decades of the Soviet Union witnessed a deliberate attempt to eradicate religion in the pursuit of a secular communist state.[23] When the Bolsheviks seized power in 1917, the elimination of religious belief was a core element of their revolutionary program. This was not accidental or incidental; it was seen as an essential aspect of the new state that was to come into being. While some areas of the Soviet Union enjoyed relative freedom in matters of religion at times, this was more due to inefficiency in the execution of central directives.

Churches were closed; priests imprisoned, exiled or executed. On the eve of the Second World War there were only 6,376 clergy remaining in the Russian Orthodox Church, compared with the prerevolutionary figure of 66,140. The most significant period of executions of priests was 1937-1938. On February 17, 1938, alone, fifty-five priests were executed. In 1917, there were 39,530 churches in Russia; in 1940, only 950 remained functional. The remainder had been closed, converted for secular use or destroyed, often by dynamiting.

In one of his more bizarre creedal statements as an atheist, Dawkins insists that there is "not the smallest evidence" that atheism systematically influences people to do bad things.[24] This is an astonishing, naive and somewhat sad statement. Dawkins is clearly an ivory-tower atheist, disconnected from the real and brutal world of the twentieth century. The facts, as we have just seen, are otherwise.

Similarly, Dawkins's puzzling remark "I do not believe there is an atheist in the world who would bulldoze Mecca—or Chartres, York Minster, or Notre Dame," says more about his personal credulity than the reality of things.[25] Similar outrages to those which took place in the Soviet Union are detailed in the postwar history of the German Democratic Republic. Surely Dawkins knows about the dynamiting of the University Church in Leipzig on the orders of the atheist authorities in 1968? Completed in 1240, this architectural masterpiece was demolished to avoid the awkwardness of having to tolerate symbols of the divine in the new "Karl Marx Platz" (now happily renamed the "Augustinerplatz," following the collapse of this grim and miserable Marxist state, which embodied precisely the austere dogmatic atheism that some seem to regard as an intellectual virtue). Dawkins's special pleading that atheism is innocent of the violence and oppression that he associates with religion is simply untenable and suggests a significant blind spot.

Let me give an example from the pen of an Oxford scholar, who comes to very different conclusions to those asserted (for they are certainly not *argued*) by Dawkins. In his outstanding study of the Romanian Christian dissident intellectual Petre Tutea (1902-1991), Alexandru Popescu documents the physical and mental degradation Tutea suffered as part of systematic persecution of religion in Romania during the Soviet era until the downfall and execution of Nicolae Ceausescu.[26] During this period, Tutea spent thirteen years as a prisoner of conscience and twenty-eight years under house arrest. His personal story is enormously illuminating for those who want to understand the power of religious faith to console and maintain personal identity under precisely the forms of persecution that Dawkins asserts do not exist.

Dawkins gives every impression of being in denial about the darker side of atheism, making him a less than credible critic of religion. He has a fervent, unquestioning faith in the universal goodness of atheism, which he refuses to subject to critical examination. Yes, there is much that is wrong with contemporary religion and much that needs to be reformed. Yet the same is also true of atheism, which still needs to subject itself to the self-searching intellectual and moral criticisms that religious systems are willing to direct against themselves. Why is it that so many atheists apply moral standards to their critique of religion that they seem reluctant to apply to atheism itself? It has often been pointed out that the new atheism applies one set of evidential criteria to its own beliefs and a more rigorous and demanding set to those of its opponents. Is the same also true of its moral critiques of religion?

THE PROBLEM OF HUMAN NATURE

Secular humanism insists on the goodness of human nature. Yet this is an unevidenced belief, which seems empirically incompatible with the violence and horrors of human history. The reality here is clearly that human beings are capable of both good and ill, moral excellence and violence—and that *both* these may be provoked by worldviews, whether religious or otherwise. It is not a comfortable insight, but one that alerts us to the shortcomings and dangers of identifying any one people group as the source of violence and the ills of humanity. This facile approach may facilitate scapegoating; it hardly advances the cause of civilization.

Furthermore, Dawkins fails to appreciate that when a society rejects the idea of God, it tends to transcendentalize alternatives—such as the ideals of liberty or equality. These now become quasi-divine authorities that none are permitted to challenge. Perhaps the most familiar example of this dates from the French Revolution, at a time when traditional notions of God were discarded as obsolete and replaced by transcendentalized human values.

Madame Rolande was brought to the guillotine to face execution on trumped-up charges in 1792. As she prepared to die, she bowed mockingly toward the statue of liberty in the Place de la Révolution and uttered the words for which she is now remembered: "liberty, what crimes are committed in your name!" Her point is simple, and I believe it to be irrefutable. All ideals—divine, transcendent, human or invented—are capable of being abused. That's just the way human nature is. And knowing this, we need to work out what to do about it, rather than lashing out uncritically at religion. The problem lies in human nature. The Christian doctrine of original sin has a lot to say about this significant failure of humanity to live up to its ideals.

IN-GROUPS AND OUT-GROUPS

This line of thought may be developed further. Suppose Dawkins's dream were to come true and religion were to disappear. Would that end the divisions within humanity? And the violence that ensues from them? Certainly not. Such divisions are ultimately social constructs that reflect the fundamental sociological need for communities to self-define and identify those who are "in" and those who are "out"; those who are "friends" and those who are "foes." The importance of binary opposition in shaping perceptions of identity has been highlighted in recent years, not least on account of the major debate between different schools of critical thought over whether such oppositions determine and shape human thought or are the outcome of human thought.

The binary oppositions that are held to have shaped modern Western culture include the pairs male-female and white-black. Group identity is often fostered by defining "the other" as an enemy—as, for example, in Nazi Germany, with its opposition Aryan-Jew. At times this binary opposition is defined in religious terms—as in Catholic-Protestant or believer-infidel.

This clearly points to religion, at least in theory, as a potential catalyst for rage and violence in some contexts. In concurring, Dawkins makes a significant concession in recognizing the *sociological* origins of division and exclusion. "Religion is a label of in-group/out-group enmity and vendetta, not necessarily worse than other labels such as skin colour, language, or preferred football team, but often available when other labels are not."[27] In other words, religion is only part of the problem—a judgment that few would find questionable. Yet even here, Dawkins's core antireligious beliefs lead him to some problematic judgments.

Dawkins assumes that the formation of in-groups and out-groups is potentially divisive and dangerous, and ought to be discouraged or prevented. Dawkins thus critiques Jesus of Nazareth for encouraging in-groups. He does not appear to know about Christ's command to love enemies, nor the inclusivism of the parable of the good Samaritan, to mention only the most obvious responses to this whimsical criticism. But at least it is clear that Dawkins is critical of the formation of in-groups and hence of the role of religion in causing such divisions.

It is therefore ironic, to say the least, that Dawkins and others now associated with the new atheism, such as Daniel Dennett, have encouraged the formation of precisely the same in-groups and out-groups by their unwise endorsement of the notion of "Brights" in 2003. For those who missed this diverting episode in American cultural history, a Bright was defined as someone who holds "a naturalistic worldview," which is "free of supernatural and mystical elements."[28]

Just as *gays* was seen as a better word to designate homosexuals, *Brights* was coined as a term for atheists. Except the choice of the term *Bright* turned out to be a public relations disaster, reeking of intellectual and cultural arrogance. If atheists were really so smart, how could two of their leading representatives fail to see that the "Brights" label would backfire so spectacularly?

When launching the Bright movement in the *New York Times* back in 2003, Dennett insisted that telling people that he was a Bright was "not a boast but a proud avowal of an inquisitive world view." Well, that's not how anyone else saw it. The opposite of Bright is dim, a mildly offensive word that translates as "stupid." By choosing to use the label Bright, atheists were widely seen to be claiming to be smarter than everyone else. As ABC's commentator John Allen Paulos remarked, "I don't think a degree in public relations is needed to expect that many people will construe the term as smug, ridiculous, and arrogant."[29]

It may have been a public relations disaster; nevertheless, the idea of Brights is completely consistent with the new atheist metanarrative. According to this controlling set of ideas, people who believe in God are intellectually and morally deficient. The atheist is the *Übermensch*, someone who is able to transcend the limitations of the human condition that cause less intelligent and discerning individuals to believe in God. To its critics this comes across as nauseatingly arrogant; within the new atheist movement itself, as I have discovered from numerous conversations, it is seen as self-evidently true. Outsiders are fools or knaves; true enlightenment is only found within its hallowed walls. Believing that the rest of humanity are deluded does, I fear, generate a certain unpleasant smugness on the part of these "true believers."

The notion of the Bright, however arrogant and smug it may be, is an essential element of the new atheist worldview. The new atheism vigorously asserts the fundamental moral and intellectual autonomy of humanity. Human beings are intelligent and rational beings who can shake off superstitious beliefs and exult in the triumph of reason and science. But where do these beliefs come from? If there is no God, it follows that religion is the creation of human beings. Hitchens and Dawkins excoriate what they see as the delusional, irrational and immoral lies of religion. Yet, from their atheist perspective, these ideas were invented by human beings—the same human beings who they exult as models of rationality and morality. Hitchens appeals to human rationality and morality in making his case for atheism, yet that same rationality and morality gave rise to religious ideas and values, which he regards as degenerate, pathological and oppressive.

Religion is the serpent in the rationalist garden of Eden, the seducer of otherwise reasonable people. The contradictions and failures of recent "enlightened" human history— which include the awkward arrival of Nazism and Stalinism, not to mention weapons of mass destruction—are put down, somewhat implausibly, to the resurgence of religion. Not even the rhetorical skills of the greatest new atheists have been able to weave Stalinism into their narrative of the obstinate persistence of religious belief. The real problem for secular rationalists is that having made human beings the "measure of all things" (Alexander Pope), they find themselves embarrassed by the wide range of beliefs human beings have chosen to hold—most notably, a widespread belief in God. If belief in God is a human invention, and if the crimes committed in the name of religion are thus of human origin, humanity appears to be rather less rational than the new atheist worldview allows. The new atheism criticizes religion as the enemy of humanity, hoping that nobody will notice that their own theory holds it to be a human creation. You don't need to be very bright to make this connection.

The only way of getting out of this impasse is by dividing humanity into two groups: those who, from an atheist perspective, are able to break free from the thrall of religion, and those who remain locked in its lethal embrace. The former, of course, are the Brights, and the latter the deluded fools who believe in God. Sure, it's arrogant and nasty. But how else can Hitchens and his colleagues escape from the impasse of the human origins of religion? If religion is evil, and religion is a human invention, what does this say about the humanity that Hitchens exalts as possessing supreme rational and moral authority? There's only one way out of this mess, and it's the invention of the Bright. If the Bright didn't exist, atheism would need to invent it.

My concern, however, is not the intellectual smugness, cultural arrogance or political foolishness of the new atheism at this point, but its fundamentally divisive nature. This crude belief system divides the world between the "Brights" and the "dims," creating a damaging polarity, which the new atheism asserts is the characteristic of religion. Atheism, it seems, is just as bad as its alternatives in this respect, having now added intellectual snobbery to its vices and nothing obvious to its virtues.

CONCLUSION

We need realism in any discussion about religion and its alternatives. It is a quality found in the writings of Michael Shermer, president of the Skeptics Society, who made the significant point that religions have been implicated in some human tragedies, such as holy wars. Indeed, this is what history tells us. But Shermer goes on to emphasize that there is clearly a significant positive side to religion:

> However, for every one of these grand tragedies there are ten thousand acts of personal kindness and social good that go unreported. . . . Religion, like all social institutions of such historical depth and cultural impact, cannot be reduced to an unambiguous good or evil.[30]

This is also what history tells us. Only someone who offers a highly selective or prejudicial reading of history could argue otherwise. Yet that is precisely the selectivity we find in the new atheist metanarrative.

The pejorative and hostile attitude toward religion on the part of the new atheism asserts that it is a universal, unambiguous evil, which is a dangerous threat to civilization. Yet just where is the balanced and judicious analysis that Shermer rightly demands? Why is it so conspicuously absent? I fear the answer is simple: because it doesn't make for the slick and simple sound bites that will reassure the godless faithful at a time of religious resurgence. True atheist believers may be relatively few, but at least they can console themselves that they are "bright."

Secular humanism appeals to the best of humanity in defining itself. So why should it not also examine the best in religion in defending itself? Of course religion can go wrong, but so can science. The forms of "social Darwinism" developed in Nazi

Germany are an abomination—but I am perfectly prepared to accept that this is bad science.[31] Both science and religion can spawn monsters. But they need not, nor are they to be judged by their pathological forms. As Voltaire (1694-1778) pointed out in his *Treaty on Toleration* (1763), "Superstition is to religion what astrology is to astronomy—the very foolish daughter of a very wise mother."[32]

The belief that religion poisons everything is simply childish. Of course religion can lead to violence and evil. But so can politics, race and ethnicity—and an aggressive and dismissive atheist worldview. In his *Treaty on Toleration*, Voltaire argued that we should not tolerate intolerance. What then of the aggressive intolerance of religion that some fanatics now seem to see as an intellectual virtue? All of us who are concerned for the creation and preservation of a human civil society want to put an end to discrimination, violence and oppression. Yet the new atheist attempt to demonstrate that religion is intrinsically and necessarily evil has led its many critics to conclude that it uses history simply as a weapon against religion, rather than as a means of illuminating the problems that we face. Surely the time has come to stop this implausible discriminatory stereotyping and deal with the real problems faced by the world?

ATHEISM AND
THE ENLIGHTENMENT

Reflections on the Intellectual Roots
of the New Atheism

IN OCTOBER 2005, ON THE EVE OF the appearance of
the new atheism, the World Congress of the International
Academy of Humanism took place in upstate New York.[1] Its
theme? "Toward a New Enlightenment." To judge from the
conference publicity, its organizers had no doubt of the urgency
of their theme. Religion was regaining the ascendancy. A new
dark ages was about to descend on the human race. The speak-
ers—who included Richard Dawkins and Sam Harris—addressed a series of topics reflecting concerns arising from the
renewed global interest in religion. Humanism holds the answers to the world's dilemmas. "We are facing a new dark ages.
Can we learn from the lessons of the British and French Enlightenment and help to bring about a New Enlightenment?"

The godfather of the new atheism is Paul Kurtz (born 1925),

one of America's most prominent secular humanists,[2] who played a leading role in articulating the vision of this Congress. Kurtz was instrumental in reshaping American humanism in a specifically secular direction during the late 1970s and early 1980s, largely by suppressing its historic religious origins and continuing religious associations and commitments. The original American "Humanist Manifesto" (1933) made specific approving reference to religious humanism.[3] Kurtz vigorously advocated more secular forms of humanism and formed the "Council for Secular Humanism" to lobby for a change in direction of the American Humanist Association. He was one of the two primary authors of "Humanist Manifesto II" (1973), setting out a vision for a form of humanism that was systematically emptied of religious possibilities and affirmations.

This insistence on humanism as a secular and secularizing movement represents a radical move away from the noble philosophy of the Renaissance, the great movement of the fourteenth and fifteenth centuries which brought about cultural renewal and regeneration throughout Europe.[4] Yet the term *humanism* was never used to refer to a secularizing, godless movement. Rather, it was about the affirmation of the importance of eloquence, especially through a return to the great sources of classical period—ancient Rome and Athens. Christian humanists, such as the great Erasmus of Rotterdam, developed programs for the renewal of the church, based on a return to the ideas and practices of the New Testament.[5] Erasmus himself produced the first printed edition of the Greek text of the New Testament and published significant commentaries on many of its books.[6] The use of the term *humanism* to refer to a movement that is atheist, secularizing and antireligious dates from the twentieth century, and represents a major distortion of the original sense of the term, as used by the writers and artists of the Renaissance.

The new atheism, however, has little interest in the historical origins of humanism or its original religious roots. This movement has hijacked the term *humanism* and uses it to designated an aggressively secularizing program that would have seemed totally alien to the writers of the Renaissance. The leading themes of this secularized humanism can be seen clearly stated in an editorial Kurtz published in his *Free Inquiry* magazine in advance of the World Congress. There was, Kurtz declared, an urgent and pressing need for a "New Enlightenment."[7] The original Enlightenment, he argued, set out to abolish "religious superstition and dogmatism, hidebound social traditions, and repressive morality." After listing the Enlightenment's many achievements with an enthusiasm unsullied by any awkwardness of historical realism, he comes to his core argument: "Unfortunately, there has been a massive retreat from Enlightenment ideals in recent years, a return to pre-modern mythologies." This must be opposed and reversed!

So what is this "Enlightenment"? And why does it have such appeal for modern secular humanism? The term *Enlightenment* is often used to refer to a period in the history of Western culture from about 1750 that placed an emphasis on the capacity of human reason to make sense of reality. This idea, of course, is found in classic Greek philosophy, as it is in most Christian philosophy. Enlightenment writers, however, took it a stage further. Where earlier writers saw human reason as a fallible yet helpful tool for *discovering* truth, many Enlightenment writers saw it as a tool for *determining* truth.[8] If something cannot be rationally proved, it is to be deemed as "irrational."

Now everyone agrees that we need to look at our own beliefs
critically and make sure that we are persuaded of their reliability. Yet in its quest for reliable knowledge, the Enlightenment
ended up setting standards of rational proof that were virtually
impossible to achieve. It is highly significant to note that Kurtz
himself regularly emphasizes the importance of "rationality,"
interpreting this not in the cautious sense used by classic Greek
philosophy but in the more ambitious terms associated with
some sections of the Enlightenment which held that all beliefs
must be capable of being proved.[9]

So who does Kurtz identify as the enemies of the Enlightenment? In terms worthy of the best conspiracy theorist, Kurtz
wrote darkly of "powerful forces eager to overthrow the basic
premises of the Enlightenment." Religion is resurgent and
must be opposed! His greatest scorn, interestingly, seems to be
directed toward the "vulgar post-modernist cacophony of
Heideggerian-Derridian mush." A new global ethic is required,
based on principles "drawn from scientific inquiry and philosophical rationality." Those who challenge the Enlightenment
are portrayed, using a depressingly superficial rhetoric of dismissal, as the enemies of reason and science, or the appeasers of
superstition and prejudice.

Kurtz's piece is as historically important as it is historically
lightweight, as it can be seen as presaging the core themes of
the new atheism, particularly as found in the writings of Richard Dawkins and Christopher Hitchens. Most media interest
has focused on their withering ridicule of religion as toxic superstition; after all, this makes for good headlines. Yet the media has been virtually silent over the other leading features of
Kurtz's program for a "New Enlightenment"—most notably,
his critique of postmodernism as irrational nonsense and a vig-

orous reaffirmation of the ethical and social vision of the Enlightenment.[10]

It is not difficult to see how a plausible link can be suggested between the rise of modernity and that of atheism. The Enlightenment's quest for intellectual and social liberation, when linked with the social and cultural situation of Western Europe, often took the form of a critique of belief in God and of the church as an institution. Both were held by some Enlightenment thinkers (though in different ways) to represent a challenge to human autonomy. Indeed, historians of modern atheism often interpret it as an integral aspect of the Enlightenment project.[11] These issues urgently need fuller analysis if we are to gain an understanding of the cultural factors which led to the emergence of the new atheism in the first place, and shape its reversionary appeal to the Enlightenment in the second.

In this chapter I want to look at the Enlightenment in ways that are unlikely to please the advocates of the new atheism. Much criticism has already been directed against the extraordinary selectivity that characterizes Dawkins's and Hitchens's critique of religion. The well-known failings of faith are trenchantly asserted as if that settled the matter. In most trials it is customary for the defense to be represented. But not, it seems, here. As Terry Eagleton commented, with a sarcasm reflecting his obvious exasperation at the *God Delusion's* risible caricatures of religion:

> Such is Dawkins's unruffled scientific impartiality that in a book of almost four hundred pages, he can scarcely bring himself to concede that a single human benefit has flowed from religious faith, a view which is as *a priori* improbable as it is empirically false.[12]

But rather than focus on this extraordinary partisan bias, let us consider the equally extraordinary selectivity evident in the appeal to the Enlightenment characteristic of the new atheism. We find the Enlightenment presented as a lost golden age, a time of intellectual prosperity and social progress. Small wonder that Hitchens yearns to return to it. But is this vision sustainable? Is not the historical reality of the Enlightenment rather more troubling? In what follows I want to offer an account of the Enlightenment that celebrates its virtues but also highlights its failures and problems. I shall do this in dialogue with three leading critics of the Enlightenment: the influential British philosopher Alasdair MacIntyre, the literary and cultural critic Terry Eagleton, and the Polish philosopher and intellectual historian Leszek Kolakowski (1927-2009).

SUBJECTING THE ENLIGHTENMENT TO CRITICAL HISTORICAL INQUIRY

One of the more puzzling features of the new atheism is its dogmatic affirmation of the excellence of the Enlightenment. Yet this bold claim is simply asserted, using diversionary rhetorical flourishes and prejudicial historical caricatures to cover up its decidedly skimpy evidential basis. These sound bites never become serious historical arguments. Yet serious historical inquiry is absolutely necessary, not least on account of the new atheism's proposed reshaping of the future after its likeness.

In his 1986 Jefferson Lecture, titled "The Idolatry of Politics," Kolakowski commented: "We learn history not in order to know how to behave or how to succeed, but to know who we are."[13] Kolakowski, while carefully acknowledging the good political and social outcomes of the Enlightenment project, insists on telling the whole story. Unlike Christopher Hitchens, he insists on drawing attention to its darker side, so easily overlooked by its apologists, lifting the veil on what the new atheism would prefer to remain concealed. For example, Kolakowski notes with concern that particular sections of the Enlightenment came to believe that certain truths had been established beyond question. On account of this hubris, he argues, Stalinism, Nazism, Maoism and "other fanatical sects" became inevitable.

These comments are especially important on account of Kolakowski's intellectual background. By the late 1940s it was obvious that Kolakowski was one of the most brilliant Polish minds of his generation. Although initially strongly committed to Marxism-Leninism, he became disillusioned with its intellectual failings and political excesses. His "revisionism" led to his expulsion from the Polish Communist Party and the loss of his teaching position at the University of Warsaw. He settled in the West, where he offered penetrating critiques of the naive assumptions that he saw as underpinning many Enlightenment ideas.

Kolakowski's point about truth is familiar to postmodern critics of the Enlightenment, who argue it offers a totalizing view of things, with the potential for fostering oppression and violence. Kolakowski's analysis of the history of the modern era exposes its complexities, challenging the simplistic narrative of progress and ascent found in Paul Kurtz. Instead of Kurtz's utopian idealism, we find a sobering realism about the human condition.

More recently, Terry Eagleton describes the Enlightenment dream of "untrammeled human progress" as a "bright-eyed superstition,"[14] a fairy tale which lacks any rigorous evidential base. "If ever there was a pious myth and a piece of credulous superstition, it is the liberal-rationalist belief that, a few hiccups

apart, we are all steadily en route to a finer world." The myth of
a lost golden age, it seems, persists in this most unlikely of quar-
ters. Yet we are surely called to question fictions about both
human individuals and society, even if these fictions are deeply
embedded within the secular Western mindset.

The new atheism often accuses those who believe in God of
holding on to "unevidenced beliefs," in contrast to the rigorously proven factual statements of enlightened atheists. Yet
what of its own unevidenced belief in human progress? Eagleton dismisses this myth as a demonstrably false pastiche, a luminous example of "blind faith."[15] What rational soul, Eagleton asks, would sign up to such a secular myth, which is obliged
to treat such human-created catastrophes as Hiroshima, Ausch-
witz and *apartheid* as "a few local hiccups" that in no way discredit or disrupt the steady upward progress of history? The
difference between Christianity and the new atheism seems to
lie in their choice of so-called unevidenced beliefs and controlling myths. Neither can be proved, nor even disproved; this,
however, does not prevent us from making an adjudication as to
which appears to be the more reliable and compelling.

Kolakowski saw history as a mirror in which human identity
was disclosed. We study history, as previously noted, so that we
might "know who we are." History, however, does not disclose
the simple *Übermensch* that Kurtz would like us to acknowledge. In fact, Kolakowski's reading of the history of modernity
leads him to the conclusion that the concept of original sin offers at least a partial explanation for humanity's darker side.[16]

As a species, humanity may indeed have the capacity for
good; this seems matched, however, by a capacity for evil. A
recognition of this profound ambiguity is essential if we are to
avoid political and social utopianism, based on naive, ideologi-

cally driven, nonempirical value judgments about human nature. As the great novelist J. R. R. Tolkien wrote so presciently in 1931, on the eve of the rise of Nazism, a naive view of humanity leads to political utopianism, in which "progress" potentially leads to catastrophe.[17]

> I will not walk with your progressive apes,
> Erect and sapient. Before them gapes
> the dark abyss to which their progress tends.

Nobody yet knew of the depths of depravity and cruelty that would be created by the rise of Nazism and Stalinism in the 1930s. Yet Tolkien saw something that most Enlightenment writers failed to see—that everything rests on the moral character of human beings. Technological developments can be used to cure or to kill. Sadly, the choice is made by human beings, and the choices they make can be disastrous. As Theodore Adorno wrote, more in sorrow than in anger, human progress seemed to be measured by the weapons it used to kill and maim other human beings. It is profoundly uncomfortable to think of human progress in terms of evolution from a sling to an atom bomb.

RECOGNIZING THE FAILINGS OF REASON

Kolakowski rightly acknowledges that the Enlightenment can be seen as a passionate quest for true, reliable knowledge. This quest is something that all can admire, in principle. But can our admiration extend beyond the principle to include its attempted implementation? I continue to find myself inspired by John Locke's famous words in his letter to William Molyneaux, dated January 10, 1697: "I know there is truth opposite to falsehood, that it may be found if people will, and is worth the seeking, and is not only the most valuable, but the pleasantest thing in the world."[18] Yet can reason and science deliver such reliable judgments?

An important criticism of the Enlightenment at this point is to be found in the writings of Alasdair MacIntyre. The Enlightenment agenda is here presented as something that is to be honored and respected. Yet for MacIntyre there is a serious problem. The Enlightenment quest for a universal foundation and criterion of knowledge faltered, stumbled and finally collapsed under the weight of a massive accumulation of counterevidence. It simply could not be done; the vision simply could not be achieved. MacIntyre's historical research into the outcomes of the Enlightenment project convinced him that its legacy was an ideal of rational justification, which it proved impossible to attain in practice.[19] The goal it set out to pursue was fundamentally correct; the problem was that its methods and resources could not ultimately sustain that quest. The pursuit of truth can hardly be abandoned because one particular strategy is now recognized to have failed; the point is to find new strategies or modify existing ones.

This may seem a harsh judgment. It may be softened, of course, by pointing out that the excessive confidence in the capacity of pure reason found in Descartes, Spinoza, Leibniz and Wolff was subjected to a penetrating critique by writers of the late Enlightenment, especially Kant. As Mark Chapman rightly notes:

> Alongside such triumphalist rationalism there were also those strands which aimed to set *limits* to human reason. . . . Although human reason may have been defined as supreme, in the sense that no other authorities were allowed, there were at the same time limits set to the extent to which human reason could be sovereign.[20]

Kolakowski illustrates Chapman's point superbly. His disarmingly frank critique of the very limited achievements of philosophical reasoning goes far beyond a critique of the inflated notions of rationality entertained within some sections of the Enlightenment, and extends to the philosophical enterprise in general:

> For centuries philosophy has asserted its legitimacy by asking and answering questions inherited from the Socratics and pre-Socratics: how to distinguish the real from the unreal, true from false, good from evil. . . . There came a point, however, when philosophers had to confront a simple, painfully undeniable fact: that of the questions which have sustained European philosophy for two and a half millennia, not a single one has been answered to general satisfaction. All of them, if not declared invalid by the decree of philosophers, remain controversial.[21]

Yet Kolakowski's critique of reason goes further than this. He insists that the human need for religion cannot be "excommunicated from culture by rationalist incantation." Human beings, he argues, do not live by reason alone. Life is more complex than rationalism allows. For Kolakowski reason has its limits and can never displace the deeper level of engagement with reality that is of the essence of religious belief and practice. The rationalist lives in an impoverished, restricted world, defined by what reason alone can prove. Yet beyond those restrictions lies a whole new vibrant world awaiting discovery and disclosure. It does not defy or contradict reason; it simply lies beyond its scope. Kolakowski encourages us to trespass into forbidden pastures, to transgress boundaries, to defy arbitrary limits. Paul Kurtz writes darkly of sinister and "powerful forces eager to overthrow the basic premises of the Enlightenment." Maybe some of those premises need to be challenged. And Kolakowski is much better placed to make that judgment than Kurtz. *Kurtz, you idiot !*

THE REEMERGENCE OF THE TRANSCENDENT

A frequent theme of new atheist writings is that of the inevitability of secularism. Religion is outmoded, a relic of a more credulous age. The future is secular; the erosion of religious belief and presence is simply a matter of time. We should embrace the future now instead of waiting for history to take its inevitable course. It is a familiar argument involving the same conflation of fact and value characteristic of Marxism.[22] Where Marx proclaimed the historical inevitability of socialism, the new atheism proclaims that of secularism.

Marx's proclamation was prophetic rather than scientific. The new atheists, however, believe that their declaration that religion is on its way out is scientific, resting on sound social analysis. Yet the idea of "historical inevitability" is a sociological judgment that has little to do with what is intellectually or morally right or wrong.[23] Whether a sociological development is "inevitable" has little bearing on whether it is right. In any case, a given historical or cultural development may be inevitable only *as a passing historical phase*, rather than as a permanent development.

The new atheism seems wedded to precisely the same Eurocentrism that became characteristic of the Enlightenment in the eighteenth century. Western Europe is unquestionably the exception to the global resurgence of religion in personal and public life in recent years.[24] It was, after all, Western European sociologists who predicted the future secularization of the world back in the 1960s; some have even lived long enough to see their predictions shown to be hopelessly naive.[25] Yet even in

Western Europe, despite a formidable array of attempts to reduce, deconstruct, recategorize or simply evade the notion of the transcendent, it remains central to contemporary cultural and philosophical reflection.[26]

Indeed, the history of ideas suggests that the assertion of the supremacy of materialist and cold rationalist approaches to reality invariably creates a backlash, generating a new interest in the domain of faith, imagination, the feelings and especially the transcendent.[27] The quest for the transcendent is so deeply embedded in the history of human thought that it will survive political and intellectual attempts to suppress it. The reaction of Romanticism against the soulless rationality of the Enlightenment is an illustration of this trend, but it is much more widely encountered than this specific example.[28]

Kolakowski both affirms the continuing importance of the transcendent and offers an explanation of this development. "God's unforgettableness," he argued, "means that He is present even in rejection."[29] Developing this point further, Kolakowski suggests that the "return of the sacred" is a telling sign of the failure of the Enlightenment pseudo-religion of humanity, in which a deficient "godlessness desperately attempts to replace the lost God with something else." In his 1973 lecture "The Revenge of the Sacred in Secular Culture," Kolakowski further suggests that the category of sacred is essential for culture, in that it offers an ordering or organizing structure that cannot adequately be grounded in secular systems.[30]

Kolakowski's reflections on the persistence of the transcendent are clearly grounded in the Polish experience under various forms of Marxism, where any recognition of the transcendent (especially when framed in terms of God) was seen as politically unacceptable. Indeed, Kolakowski's insight can be seen to have been anticipated by the nineteenth-century German philosopher Friedrich Nietzsche, who pointed out that the metaphysical pressure to discover God never departs but lingers within human culture and experience.[31] Nietzsche's own assertion of his freedom from such "metaphysical needs" may well reflect what Peter Poellner calls the "heroic posture" of many atheists, which deliberately courts rejection and cultivates the *posture* of "standing alone."[32]

The new interest in the transcendent is easily dismissed as a deplorable lapse into irrational beliefs, reflecting an indefensible resurgence of superstition. Yet this rhetorical façade is ultimately a projection of core Enlightenment values, reappropriated by the new atheism, which aims simply to stigmatize, rather than engage with, this significant cultural development. The new interest in the transcendent can be interpreted in a number of manners—one of which is a justified reaction against the spiritual aridity of modernity.[33] Romanticism, for example, can be seen as a protest against the imaginative bleakness and spiritual dullness of a rationalist world, which limits reality to what reason can determine.

CONCLUSION

This brief engagement with the leading ideas of the Enlightenment is enough to raise serious doubts about whether the simplistic new atheist vision for a return to the Enlightenment can be sustained. Many modern writers who championed the Enlightenment have subtly altered its visions and goals, partly to relate it more clearly to their own goals and objectives, yet partly also to purge it of ideas and associations that are increasingly seen to be problematic.[34] Sociologically, the ideas of the Enlightenment must be regarded as deeply embedded in their original cultural context, and cannot simply be transplanted to a radically different environment. The ideas and values of the original Enlightenment cannot be dissociated from the historical, social and cultural context of the movement. Those schools of social theory which emphasize that ideas emerge from and are shaped by their social context have noted the historically situated character of fundamental Enlightenment themes. It is a sociological truism that there can be no going back to the Enlightenment, no uncritical transfer of its ideas and values to another moment in history, such as our own.

I need therefore to stress that Kolakowski, MacIntyre and Eagleton were all once informed and committed Marxists, fully aware of the sociological location and conditioning of ideas. All three held that the early Enlightenment was corrected by its later forms—above all, Marxism, which they saw as the flowering of this intellectual movement. I do not see this sociological sophistication, or anything remotely approaching it, in the leading writings of the new atheism.

A close reading of new atheist writings suggest that it is wedded to the idea of returning to a highly idealized and sanitized Enlightenment. Yet many would argue that this is fundamentally utopian. What if the new atheism is questing for a social and intellectual order that is little more than an illusion—a "dead time's exploded dream" (Matthew Arnold)?[35] The new atheists show no recognition of the *Standortsgebundenheit*, the historically situated character, of the Enlightenment project, leading to the curious belief that the ideas and values of the Enlightenment can somehow be transplanted into the twenty-first century, as if they were detachable from their originating context. Or that because they were so widespread, they are correct for that reason. As the Polish sociologist Zygmunt Bauman once wisely remarked, we must challenge any "prevailing ideological fashion of the day whose commonality is taken for the proof of its sense."[36] Social contexts change, and with them prevailing intellectual fashions. Cultural fashions change; what seems to be permanent and globally accepted today is discarded tomorrow.

For reasons such as these, it is deeply problematic to argue for a "New Enlightenment," a concept which assumes almost totemic significance for writers such as Christopher Hitchens. While the new atheism is more concerned to criticize others than to construct its own positive proposals, the relatively few proposals that they offer must be evaluated. Kolakowski is a powerful and informed voice in this conversation, raising serious doubts about whether the new atheism has a defensible positive vision to offer as a means of displacing religious belief and institutions. Given the defining iconic role the Enlightenment plays in shaping the atheist vision of the future, its merits must be evaluated with the same critical acumen that the new atheists direct against religion.

Toward the end of his career, as he reflected on the rise and fall of the myths and worldviews he had known and had shaped his own life, such as Marxism and the Enlightenment, Kolakowski commented: "We are living through the realization that many rationally constructed predictions made in the nineteenth century are more wrong than the so-called illusions they were trying to dispel."[37] His comment leaves us with a nagging question that cannot be ignored—namely, whether the new atheism is itself offering an illusory remedy for the tragic situation of a humanity that refuses to acknowledge its shadow side. The humanists of the Renaissance knew better than this.

It's not really surprising that the new atheism calls for a new

Enlightenment. Behind that sound bite is a piece of cultural nostalgia, a yearning for the old days when things were simpler and clearer. The new atheism's response to postmodernism is to demand a reversion to an older way of thinking, long since abandoned by intellectuals as history ruthlessly exposed their flimsy foundations and faulty reasoning. The old intellectual frameworks that gave atheism such stability in the past are crumbling. The new atheists' only solution seems to be to try to put them back up again. But culture has moved on in the West and has bypassed the Enlightenment altogether in many developing parts of the world. The new atheism shows an astonishing lack of interest in history, which it seems to treat as little more than a convenient source for its own ideas, selectively quarried. Those who so mistreat and disregard history will simply end up repeating its many past failures. The new atheism aspires to create a godless New Jerusalem; if Kolakowski is right, it will merely end up creating yet another dysfunctional utopianism.

NOTES

Introduction

[1]The novelist Dorothy L. Sayers discovered this when reading the poetry of Dante; see Barbara Reynolds, *The Passionate Intellect: Dorothy L. Sayers' Encounter with Dante* (Kent, Ohio: Kent State University Press, 1989). The intellectual radiance and spiritual insight that Sayers found in Dante's poetic vision of Christian theology is, for me, characteristic of the best Christian theologians. I hope that my borrowing the title of Reynolds's excellent study of Sayers will help convey this sense of excitement and fulfilment that theology generates and sustains in the life of faith.

[2]The phrase has also been used to designate C. S. Lewis's own approach to Christianity: see Will Vaux, *Mere Theology: A Guide to the Thought of C. S. Lewis* (Downers Grove, Ill.: InterVarsity Press, 2004), p. 17. I use the phrase in a broader sense, which embraces the theological approaches found in Lewis and their counterparts within the Christian tradition.

[3]Alister E. McGrath, *The Open Secret: A New Vision for Natural Theology* (Oxford: Blackwell, 2008).

[4]Alister E. McGrath, *A Fine-Tuned Universe: The Quest for God in Science and Theology* (Louisville, Ky.: Westminster John Knox Press, 2009).

[5]To be published as Alister E. McGrath, *Darwinism and the Divine: Evolutionary Thought and Natural Theology* (Oxford: Blackwell, 2011).

[6]Most notably, see Alister E. McGrath and Joanna Collicutt McGrath, *The Dawkins Delusion? Atheist Fundamentalism and the Denial of the Divine* (Downers Grove, Ill.: InterVarsity Press, 2007).

[7]Christopher Hitchens, *God Is Not Great: How Religion Poisons Everything* (New York: Twelve, 2007), p. 282.

[8]Terry Eagleton, *Reason, Faith, and Revolution: Reflections on the God Debate* (New Haven, Conn.: Yale University Press, 2009), p. 7.

[9]For my own small contribution to this celebration, see Alister E. McGrath, "The Shaping of Reality: Calvin and the Formation of Theological Vision," *Toronto Journal of Theology* 25 (2009): 187-204. This article is an edited version of my keynote address to the University of Toronto's Calvin Congress in June 2009.

[10]I have in mind especially Eagleton, *Reason, Faith, and Revolution* and Karen Armstrong, *The Case for God* (New York: Knopf, 2009).

[11]C. S. Lewis, "Is Theology Poetry?" in *C. S. Lewis: Essay Collection* (London: Collins, 2000), p. 21.

[12]The notion of the "interpretive community" was set out by Stanley Fish, *Is There a Text in This Class? The Authority of Interpretive Communities* (Cambridge, Mass.: Harvard University Press, 1980), pp. 147-74.

Chapter 1: Mere Theology 1

[1]This chapter is based on an introductory lecture given at St. Mellitus College, London, in September 2009 to students preparing for ordained ministry in the Church of England.

Chapter 2: Mere Theology 2

[1]This chapter is based on an introductory lecture given at St. Mellitus College, London, in September 2009 to students preparing for ordained ministry in the Church of England.

Chapter 3: The Gospel and the Transformation of Reality

[1]This chapter is based on a paper read to the Literature and Theology Seminar, Oxford University, in November 2007.

[2]Augustine of Hippo *Sermo* 88.5. See further Roland J. Teske, "Augustine of Hippo on Seeing with the Eyes of the Mind," in *Ambiguity in the Western Mind*, ed. Craig J. N. de Paulo, Patrick Messina and Marc Stier (New York: Peter Lang, 2005), pp. 72-87.

[3]Iris Murdoch, "The Sovereignty of Good Over Other Concepts," in *Exitentialists and Mystics*, ed. Peter Conradi (London: Chatto, 1998), p. 368.

[4]Augustine *Sermo* 88.5.5.

[5]For a detailed analysis of this point see Alister E. McGrath, *The Open*

Secret: A New Vision for Natural Theology (Oxford: Blackwell, 2008), pp. 115-216.

[6]Examples of works of importance to recognize and explore this point include Joseph Summers, *George Herbert: His Religion and Art* (Cambridge, Mass.: Harvard University Press, 1968); William H. Halewood, *The Poetry of Grace: Reformation Themes and Structures in English Seventeenth-Century Poetry* (New Haven, Conn.: Yale University Press, 1970); Ilona Bell, " 'Setting Foot into Divinity': George Herbert and the English Reformation," *Modern Language Quarterly* 38 (1977): 219-41; Barbara Kiefer Lewalski, *Protestant Poetics and the Seventeenth-Century Religious Lyric* (Princeton, N.J.: Princeton University Press, 1979); Elizabeth Clarke, *Theory and Theology in George Herbert's Poetry: "Divinitie and Poesy Met,"* (Oxford: Clarendon Press, 1997); R. V. Young, *Doctrine and Devotion in Seventeenth-Century Poetry: Studies in Donne, Herbert, Crashaw, and Vaughan* (Cambridge: Brewer, 2000).

[7]See Heather A. R. Asals, *Equivocal Predication: George Herbert's Way to God* (Toronto: University of Toronto Press, 1981), esp. pp. 26-29. Note also Martin Elsky, *Authorizing Words: Speech, Writing, and Print in the English Renaissance* (Ithaca, N.Y.: Cornell University Press, 1989), pp. 147-83.

[8]For example, see the analyses in Donald R. Dickson, *The Fountain of Living Waters: The Typology of the Waters of Life in Herbert, Vaughan, and Traherne* (Columbia: University of Missouri Press, 1987); Richard Leonard Caulkins, *George Herbert's Art of Love: His Use of the Tropes of Eros in the Poetry of Agape*, (New York: Lang, 1996).

[9]See Bruce A. Johnson, "The Audience Shift in George Herbert's Poetry," *Studies in English Literature* 35 (1990): 89-103. Note that I have generally used modern English spelling in reproducing Herbert's poetry.

[10]The use of *glass* in this poem may also take up some Pauline themes, most notably those found in 2 Corinthians 3:18: "But we all, with open face beholding as in a glass the glory of the Lord, are changed into the same image from glory to glory" (KJV). See Ronald G. Shafer, "George Herbert's Poetic Adaptation of St. Paul's Image of the Glass," *Seventeenth-Century News* 35 (1977): 10-11.

[11]Debora K. Shuger, *Habits of Thought in the English Renaissance: Religion, Politics, and the Dominant Culture* (Berkeley: University of California Press, 1990), pp. 91-119; Harold E. Toliver, *George Herbert's Christian*

Narrative (University Park: Pennsylvania State University Press, 1993), pp. 183-225.

[12]F. E. Hutchinson remarks that "no poem of Herbert's better shows his skill in revision": see F. E. Hutchinson, *The Works of George Herbert* (Oxford: Oxford University Press, 1941), p. 541. The three main sources for Herbert's *Temple* are the Williams manuscript (MS Jones B 62 at Dr. Williams's Library, London), the Bodleian manuscript (MS Tanner 307 at the Bodleian Library, Oxford), and the first printed edition of 1633.

[13]For comment, see Janis Lull, "Expanding 'the Poem Itself': Reading George Herbert's Revisions," *Studies in English Literature, 1500-1900* 27 (1987): 71-87. See also Lull's later study *The Poem in Time: Reading George Herbert's Revisions of the Church* (Newark, N.J.: University of Delaware Press, 1990).

[14]This is the argument of Charles Molesworth, "Herbert's 'The Elixir': Revision Towards Action," *Concerning Poetry* 5 (1972): 12-20.

[15]Helen Constance White, *The Metaphysical Poets: A Study in Religious Experience* (New York: Macmillan, 1936), pp. 181-82; Clarence H. Miller, "Christ as the Philosopher's Stone in George Herbert's 'The Elixir,'" *Notes and Queries* 45 (1998): 39-40; Yaakov Mascetti, " 'This Is the Famous Stone': George Herbert's Poetic Alchemy in 'The Elixir,' " in *Mystical Metal of Gold: Essays on Alchemy and Renaissance Culture*, ed. Stanton J. Linden (Brooklyn, N.Y.: AMS Press, 2005).

[16]Urszula Szulakowska, "The Tree of Aristotle: Images of the Philosopher's Stone and Their Transference in Alchemy from the Fifteenth to the Twentieth Century," *Ambix* 33 (1986): 53-77. For a rich collection of texts illustrating the cultural fascination with alchemy, see Stanton J. Linden, *The Alchemy Reader: From Hermes Trismegistus to Isaac Newton* (Cambridge: Cambridge University Press, 2003).

[17]The definitive study of this development remains Stanton J. Linden, *Darke Hierogliphicks: Alchemy in English Literature from Chaucer to the Restoration* (Lexington: University Press of Kentucky, 1996).

[18]Ibid., p. 106.

[19]Richard Sibbes, *A Learned Commentary or Exposition, upon the First Chapter of the Second Epistle of S. Paul to the Corinthians* (London, 1655), p. 257, cited in William Haller, *The Rise of Puritanism* (New York: Harper & Row, 1957), p. 125.

[20]Linden, *Darke Hierogliphicks*, pp. 154-92.

[21]See, for example, Vittorio Tranquilli, *Il concetto di lavoro da Aristotele a Calvino* (Milan: Ricciardi, 1979); George Ovitt, *The Restoration of Perfection: Labor and Technology in Medieval Culture* (New Brunswick, N.J.: Rutgers University Press, 1987).

[22]For attempts to identify and produce one such elixir, see Donald R. Dickson, "The Hunt for Red Elixir: An Early Collaboration Between Fellows of the Royal Society," *Endeavour* 22 (1998): 68-71.

[23]See the strident criticisms of Helen Vendler, *The Poetry of George Herbert* (Cambridge, Mass.: Harvard University Press, 1975), pp. 270-72, especially the comments concerning its "infantile vocabulary." It is normally the closing stanzas of Herbert's poems that tend to be formulaic and creedal in form (see, for example, "Jordan (I)" and "Antiphon (I)"). However, in this case, the opening stanza was the last to be composed, thus setting the creedal framework for the subsequent imaginative exploration of the issues. See further Barbara Leah Harman, *Costly Monuments: Representations of the Self in George Herbert's Poetry* (Cambridge, Mass.: Harvard University Press, 1982).

[24]The original poem includes a second stanza, omitted from versions printed in English hymnals: Not rudely, as a beast, / To run into action; / But still to make Thee prepossest, / And give it his perfection. While emphasizing the importance of "perfection," this stanza is widely regarded as inferior to the remainder of the poem.

[25]It is also possible that "glass" may designate a mirror. However, the use of the window image in "The Windows" suggests that this is more likely to be Herbert's intended application in "The Elixir."

[26]A question which arises at this point concerns the extent to which Herbert has been influenced, directly or indirectly, by Augustine of Hippo's theory of signs: see especially Richard Todd, *The Opacity of Signs: Acts of Interpretation in George Herbert's "The Temple"* (Columbia: University of Missouri Press, 1986). Todd argues that Herbert incorporates Augustine's understanding of the tension between the separate (though clearly related) worlds of *res* and *verbum* into his theory of poetic expression and poetic "reading" expressed in *The Temple*.

[27]Herbert discusses the significance of Christ's death and resurrection in many poems in *The Temple*, especially "Redemption" and "Easter."

[28]Herbert's reference to questions of social status are discussed in Cristina Malcolmson, *Heart-Work: George Herbert and the Protestant Ethic* (Stanford, Calif.: Stanford University Press, 1999). Malcolmson's essentially Marxist reading of Herbert interprets this section of "The Elixir" as a rationale for "the drudgery needed for the maintenance of the traditional order" (p. 170). This materialist reading of Herbert totally fails to locate it within the Protestant work ethic and above all the transformation of the social status of work which it accomplished.

[29]See, for example, "Easter"; "Love (III)."

[30]On this, see Andrew Walker, "Scripture, Revelation and Platonism in C. S. Lewis," *Scottish Journal of Theology* 55 (2002): 19-35.

[31]For this Christianized version of Platonism found in Augustine of Hippo, one of Lewis's theological lodestars, see Philip Cary, *Augustine's Invention of the Inner Self: The Legacy of a Christian Platonist* (Oxford: Oxford University Press, 2000), pp. 63-76.

[32]See Brad Prager, *Aesthetic Vision and German Romanticism* (Rochester, N.Y.: Camden House, 2007), pp. 2-9.

[33]C. S. Lewis, *Collected Poems* (London: HarperCollins, 1994), p. 128. For comment, see Don W. King, "Topical Poems: Lewis' Post-Conversion Poetry," in *C. S. Lewis: An Examined Life*, ed. Bruce L. Edwards (Westport, Conn.: Praeger, 2007), pp. 292-93.

[34]Note especially the references to the acquisition of the capacity to "have such sight" (1.7).

Chapter 4: The Cross, Suffering and Theological Bewilderment

[1]This chapter is based on a lecture given at the Centre for Mentorship and Theological Reflection, Toronto, Canada, in June 2009.

[2]See the discussion in Roy Baumeister, *Meanings of Life* (New York: Guilford Press, 1991).

[3]See his June 18, 1956, letter to Mary van Deussen, in which he comments that apologetics "is very wearing, and not [very] good for one's own faith. A Christian doctrine never seems less real to me than when I have just (even if successfully) been defending it" (*C. S. Lewis: Collected Letters*, ed. Walter Hooper [London: HarperCollins, 2006], 3:762).

[4]For an introduction, see Joseph E. Vercruysse, "Luther's Theology of the Cross at the Time of the Heidelberg Disputation," *Gregorianum* 57 (1976):

532-48; Dennis Ngien, *The Suffering of God According to Martin Luther's Theologia Crucis* (New York: Peter Lang, 1995). This became the topic of my first book: Alister E. McGrath, *Luther's Theology of the Cross: Martin Luther's Theological Breakthrough* (Oxford: Blackwell, 1985).

[5]Martin Luther, *D. Martin Luthers Werke: Kritische Gesamtausgabe* (Weimar: Böhlaus, 1910), 5:163: "Vivendo, immo moriendo et damnando fit theologus, non intelligendo, legendo aut speculando."

[6]Ibid., 5:176: "Crux sola est nostra theologia."

[7]Ibid., 5:179: "Crux probat omnia."

[8]Martin Luther, Heidelberg Disputation, Thesis 20: *Martin Luthers Werke*, 1:354.

[9]See here Ronald Rubin, "Descartes' Validation of Clear and Distinct Apprehension," *Philosophical Review* 86 (1977): 197-208.

[10]For excellent studies, see Robert Kolb, "Luther on the Theology of the Cross," *Lutheran Quarterly* 16 (2002): 443-66; Sybille Rolf, "Crux sola est nostra theologia. Die Bedeutung der Kreuzestheologie für die Theodizeefrage," *Neue Zeitschrift für systematische Theologie und Religionsphilosophie* 49 (2007): 223-40. The question of how Luther's theological reflections of this period are to be updated to deal with today's questions needs careful exploration: see Oswald Bayer, *Martin Luthers Theologie. Eine Vergegenwärtigung* (Tübingen: Mohr, 2003).

[11]For the importance of this point, see Richard G. Tedeschi and Lawrence G. Calhoun, *Trauma and Transformation: Growing in the Aftermath of Suffering* (London: Sage, 1995); Joanna Collicutt McGrath, "Post-Traumatic Growth and the Origins of Early Christianity," *Mental Health, Religion and Culture* 9 (2006): 291-306.

[12]Simone Weil, *Gravity and Grace* (London: Routledge, 2002), p. 81.

[13]Ibid., p. 84.

[14]There is a parallel here with Lewis, when he notes that we shall one day find ourselves in a place in which "our apparently contradictory notions . . . will all be knocked from under our feet. We shall see that there never was any problem" (Lewis, *A Grief Observed* [San Francisco: HarperCollins, 2001], p. 71).

[15]See, for example, Emmanuel Levinas, *Totality and Infinity: An Essay on Exteriority* (Pittsburgh: Duquesne University Press, 1969), p. 216. For further reflection, see John D. Caputo, "In Praise of Ambiguity," in *Ambigu-*

ity in the Western Mind, ed. Craig J. N. de Paulo, Patrick Messina and Marc Stier (New York: Peter Lang, 2005), pp. 15-34.

[16]See here the point made by Theodor W. Adorno, *Negative Dialectics* (London: Continuum, 1997), p. 24: "The system, the form of presenting a totality to which nothing remains extraneous, absolutizes the thought against each of its contents and evaporates the content in thoughts."

[17]For a fuller treatment of Luther's complex notion of the "hidden God," see Hellmut Bandt, *Luthers Lehre vom verborgenen Gott: Eine Untersuchung zu dem offenbarungsgeschichtlichen Ansatz seiner Theologie* (Berlin: Evangelische Verlagsanstalt, 1958); McGrath, *Luther's Theology of the Cross*, pp. 148-90.

[18]C. S. Lewis, *The Problem of Pain* (New York: HarperCollins, 2001), p. 91. Note also the later comment (p. 94) that pain "plants the flag of truth within the fortress of a rebel soul."

[19]Lewis, *Grief Observed*, pp. 6-7.

[20]John Beversluis, *C. S. Lewis and the Search for Rational Religion* (Grand Rapids: Eerdmans, 1985), p. 150.

[21]See Ann Loades, "C. S. Lewis: Grief Observed, Rationality Abandoned, Faith Regained," *Literature and Theology* 3 (1989): 107-21.

[22]Luther, *Martin Luthers Werke: Tischreden*, 1:16: "Sola autem experientia facit theologum."

Chapter 5: The Theater of the Glory of God

[1]This chapter is based on a talk given to graduate students at King's College, London, in March 2009.

[2]Richard Faber and Renate Schlesier, eds., *Restauration der Götter: Antike Religion und Neo-Paganismus* (Würzburg: Königshausen & Neumann, 1986); Stefanie von Schnurbein, *Göttertrost in Wendezeiten. Neugermanisches Heidentum zwischen New Age und Rechtsradikalismus* (Munich: Claudius Verlag, 1993).

[3]Ronald Hutton, *The Triumph of the Moon: A History of Modern Pagan Witchcraft* (Oxford: Oxford University Press, 2001).

[4]For a good account, see Patrick Sherry, "Disenchantment, Re-Enchantment, and Enchantment," *Modern Theology* 25 (2009): 369-86.

[5]For anticipations of this, see Abigail Lustig, "Natural Atheology," in *Darwinian Heresies*, ed. Abigail Lustig, Robert J. Richards and Michael Ruse

sity Press, 2004), pp. 69-83.

n *This Class? The Authority of Interpretive*
ass.: Harvard University Press, 1980), pp.
on this important idea, see Gary A. Olson,
and the Work of Rhetoric (Albany: State Uni-
2002).

ail in Alister E. McGrath, *A Scientific Theology:*
& T Clark, 2001), pp. 81-133.

e Philosophy of the Inductive Sciences (London: Parker,

bbes, see Richard Tuck, "The 'Christian Atheism' of
in *Theism from the Reformation to the Enlightenment*, ed.
and David Wootton (Oxford: Clarendon Press, 1992),

yers, preface to *The Mind of the Maker* (London: Methuen,

ssue with the simplistic and misleading interpretation of this
Christian themes found in Lynn White, "The Historical Roots
logical Crisis," *Science* 155 (1967): 1203-7.

ee Susan Elizabeth Schreiner, *The Theater of His Glory: Nature*
tural Order in the Thought of John Calvin (Durham, N.C.: Laby-
ss, 1991).

ture *Itinerarium Mentis in Deum* 2.

For an excellent analysis of Irenaeus's statement of the concept, see John
Behr, *Asceticism and Anthropology in Irenaeus and Clement* (Oxford: Oxford
University Press, 2000), pp. 34-85; Eric F. Osborn, *Irenaeus of Lyons*
(Cambridge: Cambridge University Press, 2001), pp. 51-141.

[15]For a theological discussion of this theme, see the magisterial study of
Julius Gross, *Geschichte des Erbsündendogmas: ein Beitrag zur Geschichte des
Problems vom Ursprung des Übels* (Munich: Reinhardt, 1960).

[16]Jam Lambrecht, "The Groaning of Creation," *Louvain Studies* 15 (1990):
3-18.

[17]John Ruskin, *Works*, ed. E. T. Cook and A. Wedderburn, 39 vols. (London: Allen, 1903-1912), 7:268.

[18]Ibid., 5:333.

[19]See, for example, William Lane Craig, "The Existence of God and the

Beginning of the Universe," *Truth* 3 (1991): 85-96.

[20]William Whewell, *Astronomy and General Physics Considered with Reference to Natural Theology*, 5th ed. (London: William Pickering, 1836), p. vi.

[21]For a good account, see Johannes Maria Stenke, *John Polkinghorne: Konzonanz von Naturwissenschaft und Theologie* (Göttingen: Vandenhoeck & Ruprecht, 2006).

[22]John Polkinghorne, *Science and Creation: The Search for Understanding* (London: SPCK, 1988), pp. 20-21.

[23]The argument is set out in detail in Alister E. McGrath, *The Open Secret: A New Vision for Natural Theology* (Oxford: Blackwell, 2008), and Alister E. McGrath, *A Fine Tuned Universe: The Quest for God in Science and Theology* (Louisville, Ky.: Westminster John Knox Press, 2009).

[24]Iris Murdoch, "The Darkness of Practical Reason," in *Existentialists and Mystics*, ed. Peter Conradi (London: Chatto, 1998), p. 198.

[25]See the influential analysis in Roy Baumeister, *Meanings of Life* (New York: Guilford Press, 1991).

[26]For a similar idea in Romantic poetry, see Thomas Weiskel, *The Romantic Sublime: Studies in the Structure and Psychology of Transcendence* (Baltimore: Johns Hopkins University Press, 1986).

[27]Joseph von Eichendorff, "Wünschelrute," in Joseph von Eichendorff, *Gedichte*, ed. P. H. Neumann (Stuttgart: Reclam, 1997), p. 32 (my translation). For comment on the theological significance of this poem, see Alister E. McGrath, " 'Schläft ein Lied in allen Dingen?' Gedanken über die Zukunft der natürlichen Theologie," *Theologische Zeitschrift* 65 (2009): 246-60. The original German text reads as follows: Schläft ein Lied in allen Dingen, / Die da träumen fort und fort, / Und die Welt hebt an zu singen, / Triffst du nur das Zauberwort.

Chapter 6: The Tapestry of Faith

[1]This chapter is based on a lecture given at the Oxford Centre for Christian Apologetics in March 2009.

[2]See, for example, Douglas John Hall, *The End of Christendom and the Future of Christianity* (Valley Forge, Penn.: Trinity Press International, 1997); Darrell Guder et al., *Missional Church: A Vision for the Sending of the Church in North America* (Grand Rapids: Eerdmans, 1998).

[3]Michael W Goheen, *"As the Father Has Sent Me, I Am Sending You": Lesslie*

Newbigin's Missionary Ecclesiology (Zoetermeer, Netherlands: Boekencen-trum, 2000).

[4]Martin Kähler, *Schriften zu Christologie und Mission. Gesamtausgabe der Schriften zur Mission*, ed. Heinzgünter Frohnes (Munich: Kaiser Verlag, 1971), p. 190: "Die älteste Mission wurde zur Mutter der Theologie."

[5]Ibid.

[6]David Bosch, *Transforming Mission: Paradigm Shifts in the Theology of Mission* (Maryknoll, N.Y.: Orbis, 1991), p. 11.

[7]For useful reflections, see John G. Stackhouse, *Humble Apologetics: Defending the Faith Today* (Oxford: Oxford University Press, 2000), pp. 131-205.

[8]Avery Dulles, *A History of Apologetics*, 2nd ed. (San Francisco: Ignatius Press, 2005), p. xix.

[9]On Pelagianism, see Alister McGrath, *Heresy: A History of Defending the Truth* (San Francisco: HarperOne, 2009), pp. 160-70.

[10]Jonathan Edwards, *Treatise on the Religious Affections* (New Haven, Conn.: Yale University Press, 1959), p. 305.

[11]Augustine of Hippo *Confessions* 1.i.1. On this point, see further Klaas Bom, "Directed by Desire: An Exploration Based on the Structures of the Desire for God," *Scottish Journal of Theology* 62 (2009): 135-48.

[12]See Corbin Scott Carnell, *Bright Shadow of Reality: Spiritual Longing in C. S. Lewis* (Grand Rapids: Eerdmans, 1999).

[13]On the cultural relevance of this point, see the classic study of Ernest Becker, *The Denial of Death* (New York: Simon & Schuster, 1973). For a theological analysis of the cross, see Alister E. McGrath, *Christian Theology: An Introduction*, 4th ed. (Oxford: Blackwell, 2006), pp. 326-59.

[14]See the discussion in David K. Clark, *Dialogical Apologetics: A Person-Centered Approach to Christian Defense* (Grand Rapids: Baker, 1993).

[15]For detailed studies of this major text, see the classic study of Robert F. Zehnle, *Peter's Pentecost Discourse: Tradition and Lucan Reinterpretation in Peter's Speeches of Acts 2 and 3* (Nashville: Abingdon, 1971). Although dated in some respects, the work remains an important analysis of the text itself and its underlying strategy.

[16]See Bertil Gartner, *The Areopagus Speech and Natural Revelation* (Uppsala: Gleerup, 1955).

[17]See Bruce W. Winter, "Official Proceedings and the Forensic Speeches in Acts 24–26," in *The Book of Acts in Its Ancient Literary Setting*, ed. B. W.

Winter and A. D. Clarke (Grand Rapids: Eerdmans, 1994), pp. 305-36.

[18]For a detailed exploration of these issues, see Alister E. McGrath, *The Open Secret: A New Vision for Natural Theology* (Oxford: Blackwell, 2008), pp. 221-315.

[19]Austin Farrer, "The Christian Apologist," in *Light on C. S. Lewis*, ed. Jocelyn Gibb (London: Geoffrey Bles, 1965), p. 26.

[20]See, for example, the approach in Rowan Williams, *Tokens of Trust: An Introduction to Christian Belief* (Norwich: Canterbury Press, 2007).

[21]Simone Weil, *First and Last Notebooks* (London: Oxford University Press, 1970), p. 147.

[22]C. S. Lewis, *Surprised by Joy* (London: Collins, 1989), p. 138.

[23]C. S. Lewis, *Rehabilitations and Other Essays* (London: Oxford University Press, 1939), p. 158.

[24]I explore this point further in Alister E. McGrath, "Erzählung, Gemeinschaft und Dogma: Reflexionen über das Zeugnis der Kirche in der Postmoderne," *Theologische Beiträge* 41 (2010): 25-38.

[25]See Roy Baumeister, *Meanings of Life* (New York: Guilford Press, 1991). Baumeister's analysis of the importance of questions of identity, value, purpose and agency is of major importance to Christian apologetics.

Chapter 7: The Natural Sciences

[1]This chapter is based on an informal presentation to science graduate students at Oxford University in May 2009.

[2]For my views on Richard Dawkins's understanding of the relation of science and religion, see Alister E. McGrath, *Dawkins' God: Genes, Memes and the Meaning of Life* (Oxford: Blackwell, 2004).

[3]Stephen Jay Gould, "Impeaching a Self-Appointed Judge," *Scientific American* 267, no. 1 (1992): 118-21.

[4]Charles A. Coulson, *Science and Christian Belief* (Chapel Hill: University of North Carolina Press, 1958), p. 22.

[5]I develop this point in Alister E. McGrath, *The Open Secret: A New Vision for Natural Theology* (Oxford: Blackwell, 2008).

[6]I explore this point in my 2009 Gifford Lectures: see Alister E. McGrath, *A Fine-Tuned Universe: The Quest for God in Science and Theology* (Louisville: Westminster John Knox Press, 2009).

[7]For a good popular account and debunking of most of these myths, see

Ronald L. Numbers, ed., *Galileo Goes to Jail and Other Myths About Science and Religion* (Cambridge, Mass.: Harvard University Press, 2009).

[8]Denis Noble, *The Music of Life: Biology Beyond the Genome* (Oxford: Oxford University Press, 2006).

[9]Richard Dawkins, *The Selfish Gene*, 2nd ed. (Oxford: Oxford University Press, 1989), p. 21.

[10]Noble, *Music of Life*, p. 13.

[11]M. R. Bennett and P. M. S. Hacker, *Philosophical Foundations of Neuroscience* (Oxford: Blackwell, 2003), pp. 372-76.

[12]Richard Dawkins, *The God Delusion* (London: Bantam, 2006), p. 196.

[13]For a detailed analysis of the difficulties, see Liane Gabora. "Ideas Are Not Replicators but Minds Are," *Biology and Philosophy* 19 (2004): 127-43.

[14]Bruce Edmonds, "The Revealed Poverty of the Gene-Meme Analogy— Why Memetics Per Se Has Failed to Produce Substantive Results," January 2005. This article was available online for some years after the *Journal of Memetics* ceased publication in 2005, but the website is no longer active. Article accessed June 17, 2009.

Chapter 8: Religious and Scientific Faith

[1]This chapter is based on the 2009 Eric Symes Abbott Memorial Lecture, delivered at Westminster Abbey, London, in May 2009.

[2]All six editions are now easily accessed online at http://darwin-online.org .uk. For those preferring to use printed sources, see Morse Peckham, ed., *The Origin of Species: A Variorum Text* (Philadelphia: University of Pennsylvania Press, 1959).

[3]William Kingdon Clifford, *The Ethics of Belief and Other Essays* (Amherst, N.Y.: Prometheus Books, 1999), pp. 70-96.

[4]William James, "The Will to Believe," in *The Will to Believe and Other Essays in Popular Philosophy* (New York: Longmans, Green, 1897), pp. 1-31.

[5]Gerald E. Myers, *William James, His Life and Thought* (New Haven, Conn.: Yale University Press, 1986), p. 460.

[6]For a good account, see Christiane Chauviré, "Peirce, Popper, Abduction, and the Idea of Logic of Discovery," *Semiotica* 153 (2005): 209-21.

[7]Charles Darwin and Nora Barlow, *The Autobiography of Charles Darwin, 1809-1882: With Original Omissions Restored* (New York: Norton, 1993), p. 118.

[8]Scott A. Kleiner, "Problem Solving and Discovery in the Growth of Dar-

win's Theories of Evolution," *Synthese* 62 (1981): 119-62, esp. 127-29. Note that substantially the same issues can be discerned in Johann Kepler's explanation of the solar system: Scott A. Kleiner, "A New Look at Kepler and Abductive Argument," *Studies in History and Philosophy of Science* 14 (1983): 279-313.

[9]William Whewell, *Philosophy of the Inductive Sciences* (London: John W. Parker, 1847), 2:36. As has often been pointed out, Whewell's theory of induction is open to criticism: see, for example, Laura J. Snyder, "The Mill-Whewell Debate: Much Ado about Induction," *Perspectives on Science* 5 (1997): 159-98.

[10]Charles Darwin, *On the Origin of the Species by Means of Natural Selection*, 6th ed. (London: John Murray, 1872), p. 164.

[11]For the best general statement of this method, see Peter Lipton, *Inference to the Best Explanation*, 2nd ed. (London: Routledge, 2004).

[12]See especially the detailed study of Elisabeth Anne Lloyd, "The Nature of Darwin's Support for the Theory of Natural Selection," in *Science, Politics, and Evolution* (Cambridge: Cambridge University Press, 2008), pp. 1-19.

[13]F. Darwin, ed., *The Life and Letters of Charles Darwin* (London: John Murray, 1887), 2:155. Hutton deserves much greater attention as a perceptive interpreter of Darwin: see, for example, John Stenhouse, "Darwin's Captain: F. W. Hutton and the Nineteenth-Century Darwinian Debates," *Journal of the History of Biology* 23 (1990): 411-42.

[14]Karl R. Popper, "Natural Selection and the Emergence of Mind," *Dialectica* 32 (1978): 339-55.

[15]Laura J. Snyder, "The Mill-Whewell Debate: Much Ado About Induction," *Perspectives on Science* 5 (1997): 159-98. Snyder elsewhere argues that Whewell's views on induction have been misunderstood and merit closer attention as a distinctive approach: Laura J. Snyder, "Discoverers' Induction," *Philosophy of Science* 64 (1997): 580-604.

[16]Christopher Hitchcock and Elliott Sober, "Prediction vs. Accommodation and the Risk of Overfitting," *British Journal for Philosophy of Science* 55 (2004): 1-34. The "weak predictivism" defended by Hitchcock and Sober has parallels elsewhere: see, for example, the careful assessment of approaches in Marc Lange, "The Apparent Superiority of Prediction to Accommodation as a Side Effect," *British Journal for Philosophy of Science* 52 (2001): 575-88; David Harker, "Accommodation and Prediction: The

Case of the Persistent Head," *British Journal for Philosophy of Science* 57 (2006): 309-21.

[17]Spencer used the phrase in his *Principles of Biology* (1864); Darwin incorporated it into the fifth edition of the *Origin*: "This preservation of favourable variations, and the destruction of injurious variations, I call Natural Selection, or the Survival of the Fittest" (Charles Darwin, *Origin of Species* 5th ed. [London: John Murray, 1869], pp. 91-92).

[18]See Michael Bulmer, "Did Jenkin's Swamping Argument Invalidate Darwin's Theory of Natural Selection?" *The British Journal for the History of Science* 37 (2004): 281-97.

[19]Charles Darwin, *On the Origin of Species by Natural Selection*, 3rd ed. (London: John Murray, 1861), p. 296.

[20]Vítezslav Orel, *Gregor Mendel: The First Geneticist* (Oxford: Oxford University Press, 1996), p. 193.

[21]Charles Darwin, *Origin of Species*, 6th ed. (London: John Murray, 1872), p. 444. This comment is not present in earlier editions of the work.

[22]See, for example, John Hedley Brooke, "The Relations Between Darwin's Science and His Religion," in *Darwinism and Divinity*, ed. John Durant (Oxford: Blackwell, 1985), pp. 40-75; Frank Burch Brown, *The Evolution of Darwin's Religious Views* (Macon, Ga.: Mercer University Press, 1986); and Nick Spencer, *Darwin and God* (London: SPCK 2009).

[23]See the Darwin Correspondence Project <www.darwinproject.ac.uk>.

[24]Stephen Jay Gould, *The Structure of Evolutionary Theory* (Cambridge, Mass.: Belknap, 2002), pp. 118-21.

[25]These comments are noted in a letter to Asa Gray, dated July 28, 1862: see F. Darwin, ed., *Life and Letters of Charles Darwin*, 3:272-74.

[26]Charles Kingsley, "The Natural Theology of the Future," in *Westminster Sermons* (London: Macmillan, 1874), p. xxiii.

[27]Ibid., p. xxv. Note also Kingsley's emphasis on divine providence in the direction of the evolutionary process (pp. xxiv-xxv).

[28]See ibid., pp. xiii-xiv.

[29]See further Randal Keynes, *Annie's Box: Charles Darwin, His Daughter and Human Evolution* (London: Fourth Estate, 2001).

[30]See the analysis in John Hedley Brooke, " 'Laws Impressed on Matter by the Creator'? The *Origins* and the Question of Religion," in *The Cambridge Companion to The "Origin of Species,"* ed. Michael Ruse and Robert J.

Richards (Cambridge: Cambridge University Press, 2009), pp. 256-74.

[31]William James, *The Will to Believe* (New York: Dover, 1956), p. 51.

[32]For the ability of Christian theology to cope with such theoretical anomalies, see Alister E. McGrath, *A Scientific Theology: 3—Theory* (London: T & T Clark 2003).

[33]For the importance of the notion of "eschatological verification," see John Hick, "Theology and Verification," in *The Existence of God* (London: Macmillan, 1964), pp. 252-74.

[34]Charles Darwin, *Origin of Species* (London: John Murray, 1859), p. 171. For examples of such "difficulties," see Abigail J. Lustig, "Darwin's Difficulties," in *The Cambridge Companion to the "Origin of Species,"* ed. Michael Ruse and Robert J. Richards (Cambridge: Cambridge University Press, 2009), pp. 109-28.

Chapter 9: Augustine of Hippo on Creation and Evolution

[1]This chapter is based on an informal lunch-time talk given to a small group of graduate students of biology in London in November 2008.

Chapter 10: Does Religion Poison Everything?

[1]This chapter is based on a public lecture given at the University of Reykjavik, Iceland, in September 2008.

[2]Richard Dawkins, *The God Delusion* (Boston: Houghton Mifflin, 2006). For a brief response to this book see Alister McGrath and Joanna Collicutt McGrath, *The Dawkins Delusion? Atheist Fundamentalism and the Denial of the Divine* (Downers Grove, Ill.: InterVarsity Press, 2007).

[3]Christopher Hitchens, *God Is Not Great: How Religion Poisons Everything* (New York: Twelve, 2007). It is instructive to compare this with Rodney Stark, *For the Glory of God: How Monotheism Led to Reformations, Science, Witch-Hunts, and the End of Slavery* (Princeton, N.J.: Princeton University Press, 2003).

[4]Sam Harris, *The End of Faith: Religion, Terror, and the Future of Reason* (New York: W. W. Norton, 2004). A fourth work is sometime mentioned in this context: Daniel C. Dennett, *Breaking the Spell: Religion as a Natural Phenomenon* (New York: Viking Penguin, 2006).

[5]Dawkins, *God Delusion*, p. 249.

[6]For an excellent philosophical critique of Dawkins, see Keith Ward, *Why*

There Almost Certainly Is a God: Doubting Dawkins (Oxford: Lion Hudson, 2008).

[7]For further exploration of this point, see Peter Harrison, *"Religion" and the Religions in the English Enlightenment* (Cambridge: Cambridge University Press, 1990); Daniel L. Pals, *Seven Theories of Religion* New York: Oxford University Press, 1996; Samuel J. Preus, *Explaining Religion: Criticism and Theory from Bodin to Freud* (New Haven, Conn.: Yale University Press, 1987).

[8]Mary Midgley, *Evolution as a Religion: Strange Hopes and Stranger Fears.* 2nd ed. London: Routledge, 2002.

[9]See Donald E. Brown, *Human Universals* (New York: McGraw-Hill, 1991), p. 48.

[10]See the important study of Jung H. Lee, "Problems of Religious Pluralism: A Zen Critique of John Hick's Ontological Monomorphism," *Philosophy East and West* 48 (1998): 453-77. Lee focuses on Sōtō Zen Buddhism, which resists pluralist as much as atheist attempts to theoretical religious reductionism, whether from a pluralist or atheist perspective.

[11]Martin Marty with Jonathan Moore, *Politics, Religion, and the Common Good: Advancing a Distinctly American Conversation About Religion's Role in Our Shared Life* (San Francisco: Jossey-Bass, 2000).

[12]Diego Gambetta, ed., *Making Sense of Suicide Missions* (Oxford: Oxford University Press, 2005).

[13]Robert A. Pape, *Dying to Win: The Strategic Logic of Suicide Terrorism* (New York: Random House, 2005).

[14]Scott Atran, "The Moral Logic and Growth of Suicide Terrorism," *Washington Quarterly* 29, no. 2 (2006): 127-47.

[15]Richard E. Wentz, *Why People Do Bad Things in the Name of Religion* (Macon, Ga.: Mercer University Press, 1993). See also Sudhir Kakar, *The Colors of Violence: Cultural Identities, Religion, and Conflict* (Chicago: University of Chicago Press, 1996).

[16]Max Horkheimer and Theodor W. Adorno, *Dialectic of Enlightenment* (New York: Seabury Press, 1972). See also Robert O. Paxton, *The Anatomy of Fascism* (New York: Alfred A. Knopf, 2004).

[17]The classic philosophical analysis of the emergence of totalitarianism in the twentieth century remains Hannah Arendt, *The Origins of Totalitarianism* (New York: Harcourt, 1951). In Arendt's analysis, religion is not

seen as a significant contributing factor to this development.

[18]For exploration of this theme, see Richard A. Burridge, *Imitating Jesus: An Inclusive Approach to New Testament Ethics* (Grand Rapids: Eerdmans, 2007).

[19]For a good discussion, see Keith Ward, *Is Religion Dangerous?* (Oxford: Lion, 2006). See further David Martin, *Does Christianity Cause War?* (Oxford: Clarendon Press, 1997).

[20]Anna Dickinson, "Quantifying Religious Oppression: Russian Orthodox Church Closures and Repression of Priests 1917-41," *Religion, State & Society* 28 (2000): 327-35. See further Dimitry V. Pospielovsky, *A History of Marxist-Leninist Atheism and Soviet Anti-Religious Policies* (New York: St. Martin's Press, 1987); and William Husband, "Soviet Atheism and Russian Orthodox Strategies of Resistance, 1917-1932," *Journal of Modern History* 70 (1998): 74-107.

[21]Joseph Frank and David I. Goldstein, eds., *Selected Letters of Fyodor Dostoyevsky*, trans. Andrew R. MacAndrew (New Brunswick, N.J.: Rutgers University Press, 1987), p. 446.

[22]Fyodor Dostoyevsky, *Devils*, trans. Michael R. Katz (Oxford: Oxford University Press, 1992), p. 691. This major work is also known by other names in English, including *The Possessed*.

[23]The literature is helpfully summarized by Dickinson, "Quantifying Religious Oppression."

[24]Dawkins, *God Delusion*, p. 273.

[25]Ibid., p. 249.

[26]Alexandru D. Popescu, *Petre Tutea: Between Sacrifice and Suicide* (Williston, Vt.: Ashgate, 2004).

[27]Dawkins, *God Delusion*, p. 259.

[28]Daniel C. Dennett, "The Bright Stuff," *New York Times*, July 12, 2003. See also Richard Dawkins, "The Future Looks Bright," *The Guardian*, June 21, 2003.

[29]Chris Mooney, "Not Too 'Bright': Richard Dawkins and Daniel Dennett Are Smart Guys, but Their Campaign to Rename Religious Unbelievers 'Brights' Could Use Some Rethinking," *Skeptical Inquirer*, March-April 2004.

[30]Michael Shermer, *How We Believe: Science, Skepticism, and the Search for God* (New York: Freeman, 2000), p. 71.

[31]See, for example, Mike Hawkins, *Social Darwinism in European and American Thought, 1860-1945: Nature as Model and Nature as Threat* (Cambridge: Cambridge University Press, 1997).

[32]"La superstition est à la religion ce que l'astrologie est à l'astronomie, la fille très folle d'une mère très sage" (Voltaire, *Treatise on Toleration*, ed. Brian Harvey [Cambridge: Cambridge University Press, 2000], p. 83). On Voltaire's alleged atheism, see Arnold Ages, "Voltaire and the Problem of Atheism: The Testimony of the Correspondence," *Neophilologus* 68 (1984): 504-12.

Chapter 11: Atheism and the Enlightenment

[1]This chapter is based on a public lecture given at Radboud University, Nijmegen, The Netherlands, in December 2009.

[2]See, for example, Paul Kurtz, *What Is Secular Humanism?* (Amherst, N.Y.: Prometheus, 2006).

[3]For an excellent account, see Mason Olds, *American Religious Humanism* (Minneapolis: University Press of America, 1996).

[4]See, for example, Charles G. Nauert, *Humanism and the Culture of Renaissance Europe*, 2nd ed. (Cambridge: Cambridge University Press, 2006). For a useful collection of essays, see Jill Kraye, ed., *The Cambridge Companion to Renaissance Humanism* (Cambridge: Cambridge University Press, 1996).

[5]James K. McConica, *Erasmus* (Oxford: Oxford University Press, 1991).

[6]See Erica Rummel, *Erasmus' Annotations on the New Testament* (Toronto: University of Toronto Press, 1986). For the impact of Renaissance humanism on the origins of the Reformation, see Alister E. McGrath, *The Intellectual Origins of the European Reformation*, 2nd ed. (Oxford: Blackwell, 2003), pp. 34-66.

[7]Paul Kurtz, "Re-enchantment: A New Enlightenment," *Free Inquiry Magazine* 24, no. 3 (2004).

[8]Louis K. Dupré, *The Enlightenment and the Intellectual Foundations of Modern Culture* (New Haven, Conn.: Yale University Press, 2004), pp. 12-17. See also Frederick C. Beiser, *The Sovereignty of Reason: The Defense of Rationality in the Early English Enlightenment* (Princeton, N.J.: Princeton University Press, 1996). The complexity and diversity of Enlightenment "rationalism" has been a major theme of recent scholarship: see, for

example, Julie Candler Hayes, *Reading the French Enlightenment: System and Subversion* (Cambridge: Cambridge University Press, 1999).

[9]For reflections on the importance of this development for Christian apologetics, see Nicholas Wolterstorff, "The Migration of the Theistic Arguments: From Natural Theology to Evidentialist Apologetics," in *Rationality, Religious Belief, and Moral Commitment*, ed. Robert Audi and William J. Wainwright (Ithaca, N.Y.: Cornell University Press, 1986).

[10]See Hitchens's plea for a "New Enlightenment": Christopher Hitchens, *God Is Not Great: How Religion Poisons Everything* (New York: Twelve, 2007), pp. 277-83.

[11]For an excellent discussion of the general issues, see Winfried Schroeder, *Ursprunge des Atheismus: Untersuchungen zur Metaphysik- und Religionskritik des 17. und 18. Jahrhunderts* (Tübingen: Frommann-Holzboog, 1998). On the French situation, see Jennifer Michael Hecht, *The End of the Soul: Scientific Modernity, Atheism, and Anthropology in France* (New York: Columbia University Press, 2003), esp. pp. 41-134.

[12]Terry Eagleton, "Lunging, Flailing, Mispunching: A Review of Richard Dawkins' *The God Delusion*," *London Review of Books*, October 19, 2006. For Eagleton's own perceptive and critical comments on this important issue, see Terry Eagleton, *Holy Terror* (New York: Oxford University Press, 2005).

[13]Leszek Kolakowski, "The Idolatry of Politics," in Leszek Kolakowski, *Modernity on Endless Trial* (Chicago: University of Chicago Press, 1990), pp. 146-61.

[14]Terry Eagleton, *Reason, Faith, and Revolution: Reflections on the God Debate* (New Haven, Conn.: Yale University Press, 2009), p. 28.

[15]Ibid., pp. 87-89.

[16]Leszek Kolakowski, "Can the Devil Be Saved?" in Kolakowski, *Modernity on Endless Trial*, pp. 75-85.

[17]J. R. R. Tolkien, "Mythopoeia," in *Tree and Leaf* (London: Harper Collins, 1992), p. 89.

[18]John Locke, *The Works of John Locke* (London: Thomas Tegg, 1823), 8:447.

[19]Alasdair MacIntyre, *Whose Justice? Which Rationality?* (London: Duckworth, 1988), p. 6. The diversity of notions of reason within the Enlightenment has led many scholars to query whether the use of the singular

term *Enlightenment* can be sustained. There seem to be several "Enlightenments"—or at least a wide range of implementations of a single Enlightenment agenda, if this can indeed be defended. See especially James Schmidt, *What Is Enlightenment? Eighteenth-Century Answers and Twentieth-Century Questions* (Berkeley: University of California Press, 1996).

[20]Mark D. Chapman, "Why the Enlightenment Project Doesn't Have to Fail," *Heythrop Journal* 39 (1998): 380.

[21]Leszek Kolakowski, *Metaphysical Horror* (Chicago: University of Chicago Press, 2001), pp. 1-2.

[22]A point made repeatedly throughout Leszek Kolakowski, *The Main Currents of Marxism*, 3 vols. (Oxford: Oxford University Press, 1976-1978).

[23]A point famously emphasized by Karl R. Popper, *The Poverty of Historicism* (London: Routledge & Kegan Paul, 1957). For comment from a (then) leading atheist writer, see Anthony Flew, "Human Choice and Historical Inevitability," *Journal of Libertarian Studies* 5 (1981): 345-56.

[24]See Grace Davie, *Europe: The Exceptional Case. Parameters of Faith in the Modern World* (London: Darton Longman & Todd, 2002).

[25]See, for example, Scott Thomas, *The Global Resurgence of Religion and the Transformation of International Relations: The Struggle for the Soul of the Twenty-First Century* (New York: Palgrave Macmillan, 2005).

[26]See the points made by Max Horkheimer in his interview with Helmut Gumnior: Max Horkheimer, *Die Sehnsucht nach dem ganz Anderen. Ein Interview mit Kommentar von Helmut Gumnior* (Hamburg: Furche-Verlag, 1971).

[27]As noted and illustrated by J. W. Burrow, *The Crisis of Reason: European Thought, 1848-1914* (New Haven, Conn.: Yale University Press, 2000), pp. 56-67.

[28]Graeme Garrard, *Counter-Enlightenments from the Eighteenth Century to the Present* (London: Routledge, 2006). Note especially the section dealing with the "return of faith and feeling" (pp. 55-73).

[29]Leszek Kolakowski, "Concern About God in an Apparently Godless Age," in *My Correct Views on Everything*, ed. Zbigniew Janowski (South Bend, Ind.: St. Augustine's Press, 2005), p. 183. For a more rigorous exploration of this theme, see Charles Taylor, *A Secular Age* (Cambridge, Mass.: Belknap Press, 2007).

[30]Leszek Kolakowski, "Revenge of the Sacred in Secular Culture," in Leszek Kolakowski, *Modernity on Endless Trial*, pp. 63-74. Theological engagement with Kolakowski at this point (or any, for that matter) is rare: for a luminous exception, see Peter Hebblethwaite, "Feuerbach's Ladder: Leszek Kolakowski and Iris Murdoch," *Heythrop Journal* 13 (1972): 143-61.

[31]Friedrich Wilhelm Nietzsche, *Human, All Too Human: A Book for Free Spirits* (Cambridge: Cambridge University Press, 1986), p. 153. For this "metaphysical need," see Tyler T. Roberts, *Contesting Spirit: Nietzsche, Affirmation, Religion* (Princeton, N.J.: Princeton University Press, 1998), pp. 49-53.

[32]Peter Poellner, *Nietzsche and Metaphysics* (Oxford: Oxford University Press, 2000), p. 9.

[33]Kolakowski, *Modernity on Endless Trial*.

[34]An excellent example of such a neoconservative reading of the Enlightenment is found in Gertrude Himmelfarb, *The Roads to Modernity: The British, French, and American Enlightenments* (New York: Knopf, 2004).

[35]Matthew Arnold, "Stanzas from the Grande Chartreuse" (1855), line 98.

[36]Zygmunt Bauman, "On Writing: On Writing Sociology," *Theory, Culture & Society* 17 (2000): 79.

[37]Leszek Kolakowski, "Man Does Not Live by Reason Alone," *New Perspectives Quarterly* 26, no. 4 (2009): 19-28.

Index

Also by A E Mc:

Why God Won't Go Away.

P. 201 > Alister + Joanna Collicutt McGrath:
The Dawkins Delusion; Atheist Fundament
alism and the Denial of the Divine.
> Alister McGrath: Dawkins' God; Genes,
Memes, and The Meaning of life.